SOURCE

Fay Sweet

SOURCE

an internet directory of modern interior design

QUADRILLE

CONTENTS

This book was inspired by curiosity. Whenever I look at pictures of amazing interiors, I want to know where the sofa came from, and the faucets, and how they got the floor to look like that? I also like to know how the architect created a new space or improved what was already there. I am not alone in my curiosity, so I have compiled this book to explore what goes into making interesting, comfortable, and livable contemporary interiors.

At the heart of *Source* is a collection of inspiring homes from around the world. I never cease to be impressed by the skills of architects, particularly their ability for 3D thinking, in fashioning new spaces as well as remodeling existing rooms; many are expert at the finishes and are fastidious over detail, with an encyclopedic knowledge of materials and products. Interior designers share many of these skills and possess impressive abilities in building color schemes, combining textures, and sourcing furnishings. *Source* is a window onto this world.

Whether your aim is to transform a room or build a house from scratch, you'll start to construct a picture in your mind of how the space will be used and how it will look. Whether you choose to hire a professional or not, it helps to have ideas about finishes and furnishings. Finding the perfect leather sofa or dining table can be a real pleasure, but it's not just the big items that count. A beautiful door will be spoiled by a miserable, uncomfortable handle. These details not only build character; they will also contribute to your enjoyment of a room.

In the choice of interior shots for *Source*, the emphasis is on a contemporary style of home with modern classic furniture and lighting, together with shelving and storage, items for kitchens, bathrooms, bedrooms, and gardens and details right down to the light switches. In recent years, coinciding with our desire to live in open-plan, uncluttered, stylish homes, there has been a growing interest in classic designs by the great Modernist heroes, including Le Corbusier, Ludwig Mies van der Rohe, and Charles and Ray Eames; many of their greatest designs are featured here. In some cases, these classic pieces are licensed to be made by just one manufacturer; however, where the copyright has expired, they may be produced by a number of companies. The websites provided are either those of the sole manufacturer or of one of the companies acknowledged to be making the best-quality versions of the design. Beware of opting for the cheapest lookalike products; you usually get what you pay for. There are, of course, copycat companies at work throughout the furnishing industry, but in the case of more recent designs by the likes of today's stars, such as Philippe Starck, Marc Newson, and Jasper Morrison, the manufacturers given here will be the sole producers of the genuine article.

As we all become more aware of the importance and pleasures of comfortable, good-looking, and practical interiors, we have become design aficionados. With the comprehensive range of products on show throughout the book, *Source* is designed to make it quicker and easier to track down exactly what you are looking for.

INTRODUCTION

se *Source*

...num inspiration and
...e interested in
...out is unique—
...howing a stunning
...e of products chosen
...ave stood the test of
...ecognized modern
...use they have the
...lassics of the future.
...architects and
...' ideas for each
...y necessary problem
...together with the
...ny items as possible
...of being captioned,
...d with descriptions of
...website of their
...the provenance of
...manufacturers of
...ested.
...' a book of its time.
...mber of us using the
...esearch and
...*Source* gives web
...easy to find
...ers, and suppliers.
...rchitect or designer,
...te, you'll be gaining
...io of work. If you are
...project, this is a
...ilding a shortlist of
...right for the job.

Increasingly, architects and designers are finding that their clients are using the web to make their choice—their websites are usually very good.

When it comes to the manufacturers, the majority of those named in *Source* export their products around the world. Almost without exception, the quality of the website designs and the level of information available are astonishingly good. This is a huge, valuable, and under-sung resource. Most sites are very good-looking and easy to navigate; many have information giving the materials and dimensions of the product and the range of finishes available. Together with looking at the range of products, it's possible to find out about the company's history, and design philosophy, information about the designers, and details of your nearest retailer.

• *Source* is designed to help you find the very best of modern design for the home; it provides a link with manufacturers, who can guide you to your nearest retailer.

• Once you have found an item you like, enter the manufacturer's website address into your computer.

• In many cases the manufacturer's central website is listed, but there may be national and regional options, too.

• After entering the ma...
website, you'll find a w...
information; many not...
the full range of produ...
information about desi...
the technical specificati...
dimensions of the prod...

• Should you encounter...
activating a website ad...
idea, as an alternative, ...
manufacturer's name in...

• Some manufacturers ...
entire collection on the...
many cases it is possible...
brochure of the full ran...

• If you decide to buy a...
many websites have a s...
main importers and dis...
different countries; the...
to find your nearest sto...

• Where the importers ...
not included, go to the ...
contact info and send a...
product you'd like and ...
and ask for your neares...

• In those cases where ...
nearby, use the e-mail f...
manufacturer for inforr...
shipping the product di...

- Comfortable seating is a must; the sofa is the key item. Take care to keep it in scale with the room, as sofas can take up a huge amount of space.

- Avoid overreliance on ceiling fixtures, which cast a watery glare; use table and floorlamps for flexibility and flattering pools of light.

- A fireplace is unnecessary with central heating, but a wonderful, inviting focal point.

- Coffee tables and occasional tables are extremely useful for cups and glasses.

- Dimmer switches quickly change the lighting levels; programmable lighting systems are an increasingly affordable luxury.

- Because living rooms are used so intensively, good storage, whether cabinets, shelving or a mixture of the two, makes it easier to tidy away books, music CDs, videos, and DVDs.

The living room is one of the most intensively used spaces in the home. It has to be flexible and adaptable throughout the day, from catching up with the breakfast news to evening dining or entertaining. Above all, this is a place to rest, away from outside pressures, so comfortable seating is an essential component. The sofa will be a facing each other suggest a waiting room; an L-shaped configuration is more social and makes it easy for people to talk together. Where space is at a premium, choose a smaller-scale sofa and a couple of armchairs. Additional seating can be provided with an upholstered bench or side chairs. Lighting is an important

LIVING ROOMS

major purchase and will set the tone of the room—a sleek black leather and chrome design has a metropolitan look; corduroy or colorful plain wool upholstery is smart and welcoming; stripes can be upbeat, while a floral pattern usually has a country feel. The arrangement of seating is crucial to the way the space is used—two sofas element in the living room, too. Because this room must accomodate many different uses, lighting should include floor, wall, and table lamps, as well as a ceiling fixture. Dimmer switches are a great idea, enabling a quick change of tempo. For real luxury, opt for a programmable system in which different settings produce different moods.

Model No. PK31 (1958) by Poul Kjærholm
□ **www.fritzhansen.com**

Breuer Sofa (1936) by Marcel Breuer
□ **www.isokonplus.com**

Model No. hm991i (1998) by David Chipperfield
□ **www.hitchmylius.com**

Club sofa (1962) by Robin Day
□ **www.loftonline.net**

Milano (1982) by Gionatan De Pas, Donato D'Urbino & Paolo Lomazzi
□ **www.zanotta.it**

Model No. 2213 (1962) by Børge Mogensen
□ **www.fredericia.com**

Sofa With Arms (1982) by Shiro Kuramata
□ **www.cappellini.it**

Tolomeo floor lamp in aluminum (1987), Michele de Lucchi & Giancarlo Fassina □ **www.artemide.com**

Superellipse Table in maple (1968), Piet Hein & Bruno Mathsson □ **www.fritzhansen.com**

DKR-2 (Dining Bikini Rod) chair in brown leather (1951), Charles & Ray Eames □ **www.vitra.com**

Met modular sofa in brown leather (1996), Piero Lissoni with S. Sook Kim □ **www.cassina.it**

Party space
by Feeny Mallindine Architects
www.feenymallindine.com

The sociable owners of this modernized turn-of-the-century house love to give parties and even enjoy small musical concerts at home. To make a space for around 30–40 guests, the architect has merged two rooms at the back of the house and added a 6ft-deep, sheer glass garden extension across the entire width of the building. The back wall of the house is supported by a single sturdy steel column. The new space is not just perfect for parties; it has the feel of a large apartment and yet is comfortable for the couple when they are alone.

1 Sheer, floor-to-ceiling doors form the front of this capacious custom-built storage wall. The wood used is sycamore, which has been given a tough, clear lacquer finish □ **for wood paneling, see the Directory of Suppliers on pages 152–55**

2 The glass used here is a low-emissivity product, which helps to control the temperature of the room. It is used in sealed panels of $\frac{5}{16}$" glass, with an $\frac{5}{16}$" air gap and then $\frac{3}{16}$" glass on the outside. The sliding door is anodized aluminum □ **for architectural glass, see the Directory of Suppliers on pages 152–55**

3 The clients wanted to have a built-in fish tank. This one is unusual because it contains salt water, which supports a great variety of fish. Salt water tanks are slightly more expensive to set up and run than their plain water counterparts □ **for aquariums and fish tanks, see the Directory of Suppliers on pages 152–55**

4 The main part of the room has an American elm floor, with Portuguese limestone in the new glass extension. The honey color of the elm sits well with the sycamore-faced cabinets. □ **for wood and stone flooring, see the Directory of Suppliers on pages 152–55** □ The elm flooring is treated with BonaKemi, a durable water-based sealant that gives the wood a natural finish □ **www.bona.com**

5 Apta Collection, Model No. 9614, coffee table by Antonio Citterio. Shown here with a wenge table top, but is also available in gray oak, brown oak, and gray and brown oak with a pickled finish □ **www.maxalto.it**

Lansdowne (2003) by Terence Woodgate
□ **www.scp.co.uk**

Zurigo (1998) by Alfredo Häberli &
Christophe Marchand □ **www.zanotta.it**

Soft Mellow (2002) by Marcel Wanders
□ **www.moooi.com**

Model No. hm61 (1998) by Nigel Coates
□ **www.hitchmylius.com**

Series 3300, Model No. 3302 (1956) by Arne Jacobsen
□ **www.fritzhansen.com**

Model No. 3321, Swan Sofa (1958) by Arne Jacobsen
□ **www.fritzhansen.com**

Lazy Working Sofa (1998) by Philippe Starck
□ **www.cassina.it**

606 Universal Shelving System (1960), Dieter Rams □ www.vitsoe.com

Parentesi suspended lamp (1970), Achille Castiglioni & Pio Manzu □ www.flos.net

Bauhaus lamp (1924), Wilhelm Wagenfeld □ www.tecnolumen.de

Model No. PK22 easy chair in natural leather (1955–56), Poul Kjærholm □ www.fritzhansen.com

Charles sofa with cream cloth upholstery (1998), Antonio Citterio □ www.bebitalia.it

Scandinavian cool
by Shideh Shaygan

www.shaygan.com

When the owners first saw this apartment in an 1880s residential building, it was dark and cluttered, but they could see the appeal of its large reception rooms. The refurbishment project involved stripping the rooms back to the bare walls, retaining as much of the fine detailing as possible, including the wood paneling and classic Scandinavian fireplace—the kakelugn—and installing new services. The grand architectural scale of the place is now the backdrop to a more contemporary style of living.

1 Original ceramic tiled fireplace, kakelugn, with decorative panels showing hand-painted water lilies □ **for architectural salvage, including fireplaces, see the Directory of Suppliers on pages 152–55**

2 BeoSound 3000 music system □ **www.bang-olufsen.com**

3 Block lamp (1996) by Harri Koskinen □ **www.designhouse2.com**

4 Coffee table designed by the architect. Constructed from white oiled oak, this unusual design incorporates built-in lighting □ **www.shaygan.com**

5 Thought to be a Danish design from the 1950s, the interlocking blonde wood tables were found in a Copenhagen secondhand store □ **for vintage furniture, see the Directory of Suppliers on pages 152–55**

6 Teardrop table lamp (1999) by British artist Anish Kapoor sits on the Danish side tables. This limited-edition lamp was part of a specially commissioned series of domestic products by sculptors created in conjunction with the Tate Gallery, London □ **www.homebase.co.uk**

7 The original herringbone-pattern oak parquet had become very dark with age and wear, but has now been sanded and treated with a natural linseed oil mixed with white pigment for a light finish □ **www.triptrap.com**

8 Fields rug by Thomas Eriksson. Hundred-percent wool rug available in various sizes and combinations of 17 colors □ **www.kasthall.se**

9 Painting from the "Walker" series (2001) by well-known contemporary Swedish artist Jan Håfström □ **www.the-artists.org**

Balzac (1991) by Matthew Hilton
□ **www.scp.co.uk**

Genni (1935) by Gabriele Mucchi
□ **www.zanotta.it**

Model No. EJ 100, Oxchair (1960) by
Hans J. Wegner □ **www.erik-joergensen.com**

Model No. EJ 96, Apollo by Foersom &
Hiort-Lorenzen □ **www.erik-joergensen.com**

Armchair 400 (1935–36) by Alvar Aalto
□ **www.artek.fi**

Club by Matthew Hilton
□ **www.scp.co.uk**

Sax (2002) by Terence Woodgate
□ **www.scp.co.uk**

Series 3300, Model No. 3300 (1956) by
Arne Jacobsen □ **www.fritzhansen.com**

Armchair 41, Paimio (1931–32) by
Alvar Aalto □ **www.artek.fi**

Classic 86 cast-iron wood-burning stove (1970) by Bent Falk □ www.rais.dk

Series 3300 sofa in black leather (1956), Arne Jacobsen □ www.fritzhansen.com

Tolomeo floor lamp in aluminum (1987), Michele de Lucchi & Giancarlo Fassina □ www.artemide.com

Model No. PK22 easy chair in black leather (1955–56), Poul Kjærholm □ www.fritzhansen.com

Tea Trolley 901 in birch with white laminate (1935–36), Alvar Aalto □ www.artek.fi

Delight in the detail
by Smith-Miller + Hawkinson Architects
www.smharch.com

The architect of this house described the design idea bluntly as "a shipping container on stilts". This is to severely downplay the elegance of the project. The timber-clad, near-rectangular building is constructed on the side of a sloping valley and stretches out into the landscape on stilts. The full wall of glass at the far end of the living room gives spectacular valley and river views. The 1,080 square feet of interior space are divided between this open-plan living room with kitchen space, two bedrooms, and a bathroom. Although the structure appears very simple, it is pervaded by an impressive attention to detail.

1 Oversized floorlamp. Similar in design to the Fortuny floorlamp by Mariano Fortuny Y Madrazo for Pallucco Italia, designed originally for use in theaters. Available with a black- or titanium-colored epoxy powder-coated base with either a black or beige lampshade □ www.palluccobellato.it

2 LC1 chair (1928) by Le Corbusier. A chromed tubular steel frame with leather seat and back and slung leather arms □ www.cassina.it

3 Oak flooring, coated with a matte sealant □ for wood flooring, see the Directory of Suppliers on pages 152–55

4 3107 chair (1955), one of the Series 7 designs, by Arne Jacobsen. One of the most widely imitated contemporary chair designs, which has been in continuous production since the 1950s □ www.fritzhansen.com

5 Valmarana dining table in ash (1971) by Carlo Scarpa, now discontinued. Other designs by Carlo Scarpa available from Bernini □ www.bernini.it

Model No. 890 (2002) by Liévore, Altherr & Molina □ **www.thonet.de**

LC2 Petit Confort (1928) by Le Corbusier, Jeanneret & Perriand □ **www.cassina.it**

Model No. 635, Red/Blue Chair (1918) by Gerrit Thomas Rietveld □ **www.cassina.it**

Boxer by Ola Rune □ **www.skandiform.com**

Ondina (1987) by De Pas, D'Urbino & Lomazzi □ **www.zanotta.it**

Breuer Armchair (1936) by Marcel Breuer □ **www.isokonplus.com**

Zurigo (1998) by Alfredo Häberli & Christophe Marchand □ **www.zanotta.it**

Model No. CH22 (1950) by Hans J. Wegner □ **www.carlhansen.com**

Poly Armchair (1967) by Robin Day □ **www.loftonline.net**

Jetmaster Universal 1200 fireplace
□ www.jetmaster.com

Armchair 402 in birch with zebra fabric (1932–33),
Alvar Aalto □ www.artek.fi

Closer to nature

by George Elphick at Elphick Proome Architects

www.eparch.co.za

This large, open, glass-walled extension has been added to the
existing structure of the architect's own family home to enhance
the connection between the interior and the stunning landscape.
The strong relationship with nature is important to the household, especially since the architect's wife runs a natural health
practice from home. In addition to this living space, a contrasting
cozy study-music room was added, along with a gallery area.
The new living space extends into the garden with the addition
of the verandah, which is shaded by the protecting "wing" of
the steel-frame roof, which swoops upward toward the forest.

1 Manila chair in polished aluminum by Amat-3. This design is ideal
for use outside because it can easily withstand rain and will not rust
□ **www.amat-3.com**

2 Zen Table in iroko wood by Empire Design. Also available in natural
ash and stained ash □ **www.empire-design.co.za**

3 Le Cube two-seater sofa in black leather and chrome tubular steel
by Pago. Also available as a single seater and three seater
□ **www.pago.co.za**

4 Coffee table on casters designed by the architect and home owner
□ **www.eparch.co.za** □ Manufactured by Exotic Furniture
□ **www.exoticfurniture.co.za**

5 In contrast to the balau timber decking outside, the floor is a
charcoal oxide-dyed, steel-troweled poured concrete floor with two-
part polyurethane gloss □ **for concrete flooring, see the Directory of
Suppliers on pages 152–55** □ Cement Floorcote oxide and sealant
by Earthcote □ **www.earthcote.co.za**

6 Burnt-orange wool rug. Similar to Fasett rug in orange 107–1007
from Kasthall □ **www.kasthall.se**

Model No. PK22 (1955–56) by
Poul Kjærholm □ **www.fritzhansen.com**

Tinto by Mårten Claesson, Eero Koivisto
& Ola Rune □ **www.offecct.se**

Coconut (1955) by George Nelson
□ **www.vitra.com**

Burghley (1923) by Lloyd Loom Studio
□ **www.lloydloom.com**

Model No. S35R (1929) by Marcel Breuer
□ **www.thonet.de**

Mono by Ola Rune
□ **www.offecct.se**

Model No. PK20 by Poul Kjærholm
□ **www.fritzhansen.com**

Model No. CH07 (1963) by Hans J. Wegner
□ **www.carlhansen.com**

Clea (1997) by Kristiina Lassus
□ **www.zanotta.it**

D:6 chair (1998), Björn Dahlström
□ www.cbidesign.se

Diamond easy chair (1950–52),
Harry Bertoia □ www.knollint.com

Garden pavilion
by Anna von Schewen Design and Architecture

www.annavonschewen.com

When Anna von Schewen was asked by her brother to create a new family home, her approach was to work from the inside out and focus on the way the house would be used. It naturally divided into three zones—a place for sleeping, a place for cooking, and a living/dining room for sharing meals with friends and enjoying the views and nature. The designer's approach is the same when creating furniture, where she starts with the body. The living area is a family and entertaining space, clad with wood on two walls and on the upward sloping ceiling, with two walls of floor-to-ceiling glass. The large expanses of glass

allow the room to stand almost like an open pavilion. The transparency of the space gives the family the close contact it wants with the surrounding landscape. The house has water on both sides, and at certain times of day, the sloping ceiling picks up animated reflections.

1 Latta easy chair (1997) by Anna von Schewen. This unusual chair is built with strips of sensuously curved laminated wood and covered with a woven fabric, so the whole chair bends and molds itself to the shape of the body □ **www.annavonschewen.com**

2 Walls and ceiling are clad in vertical wooden boards, which encourage the eye upward and make the space appear to soar. The boards add an interesting and subtle texture to the space and are painted white to keep the room feeling open and fresh
□ **for wood cladding, see the Directory of Suppliers on pages 152–55**

3 Custom-made dining table designed and made by the architect
□ **www.annavonschewen.com**

4 Like most of this structure, the floor is made from pine that has been given a light coat of whitewash □ **for wood flooring, see the Directory of Suppliers on pages 152–55**

5 EJ 220 sofa, designed and produced by Erik Jørgensen
□ **www.erik-joergensen.com**

6 Regnbågsmattan striped rug, designed by Josef Frank
□ **www.svenskttenn.se**

Model No. 3316, The Egg with footstool (1958) by
Arne Jacobsen □ **www.fritzhansen.com**

Model No. EJ 5, Corona (1961) by Poul Volther
□ **www.erik-joergensen.com**

Tipto (2004) by Peter Emerys-Roberts & Christine Harvey
□ **www.driade.com**

Model No. S411 (1932) by Thonet
□ **www.thonet.de**

Scoop (2000) by Mårten Claesson, Eero Koivisto & Ola Rune
□ **www.livingdivani.it**

Toop (2000) by Eero Koivisto
□ **www.david.se**

Glo-ball floorlamp (1998),
Jasper Morrison □ **www.flos.net**

Luminator floorlamp and uplighter (1954),
Achille & Pier Giacomo Castiglioni □ **www.flos.net**

Bestlite reading lamp (1930), Robert Dudley Best
□ **www.bestandlloyd.co.uk**

1

2

3

4

5

Stool Model No. 60 in birch (1932–33),
Alvar Aalto □ **www.artek.fi**

Lounge Chair No. 670 & Ottoman No. 671 in black leather (1956),
Charles & Ray Eames □ **www.vitra.com**

Sky High
by Simon Allford at
Allford Hall Monaghan Morris
www.ahmm.co.uk

The brief for this modest urban apartment, at the top of a late nineteenth-century, red-brick appartment house was to open up the spaces and bring in as much natural light as possible. In stripping the place back to its shell, the ceilings were removed to add to the quality of space by making the rooms taller. Roof lights were also added. Doors to small roof terraces extend the space outward. Luxurious detailing includes the use of rich walnut wood throughout for all joinery. The collection of modern classic furniture and lighting sits comfortably in this elegant setting.

1 Wall-fixed magazine rack from Paustian
□ **www.paustian.dk**

2 The credenza was constructed by a local joinery firm □ **for furniture designers and makers, see the Directory of Suppliers on pages 152–55**

3 Élan sofa in black leather by Jasper Morrison, part of a modular seating system □ **www.cappellini.it**

4 Op-la tray table (1998) by Jasper Morrison. Stainless steel base with ABS plastic tray tabletop □ **www.alessi.com**

5 Cork tiles are much underrated as a floor covering; they are natural and warm and easy to install. Suppliers are fewer in number than in the 1970s, when cork enjoyed a period of popularity, but many good flooring supply companies will have cork tiles somewhere on their product lists □ **for natural floor coverings, including cork tiles, see the Directory of Suppliers on pages 152–55**

The Matrix
□ www.verine.co.uk

Firescape by Henry Harrison
□ www.platonicfireplaces.co.uk

Firescheme by Henry Harrison
□ www.platonicfireplaces.co.uk

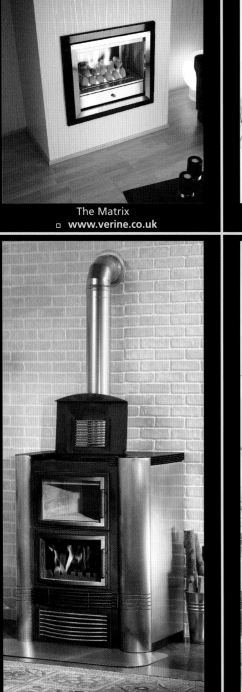

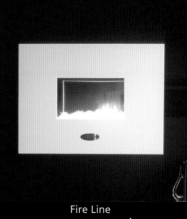

Fire Line
□ www.cvo.co.uk

The Metro
□ www.chesneys.co.uk

Jolly Mec Caldea
□ www.jolly-mec.it

Bathyscafocus by Dominique Imbert
□ www.focus-creation.com

Classic 106
□ www.rais.dk

Agorafocus ceiling suspended fireplace, Dominique Imbert □ **www.focus-creation.com**

Costanza adjustable floorlamp (1985), Paolo Rizzatto □ **www.luceplan.com**

Oxchair in black leather (1960), Hans J. Wegner □ **www.erik-joergensen.com**

Grown-up time
by Magnus Ståhl Architect

www.staahl.com

The converted attic space of this large family house is a tranquil area to which the parents can withdraw at the end of a long day. The room has been treated as simply as possible with solid oak flooring and white walls and ceiling, which is finished in painted wood planking for a light, yet warm effect. Floor-to-ceiling, metal-frame sliding doors lead on to a small terrace. There's also a guest room and shower room up here, with the shower opening directly onto the terrace.

1 The entire space is lined with wood boards, which have been painted white—the effect is charming and distantly reminiscent of log cabins, ships' interiors, or even, perhaps, a treehouse □ **for wood cladding, see the Directory of Suppliers on pages 152–55**

2 Punktlampan spot lights in aluminum by Focus Belysning. The lights protrude slightly from the ceiling. Available in four different sizes □ **www.foxdesign.se**

3 Built-in cabinets designed by the architect. The oak doors open out and then slide back into the wall. One cabinet contains a TV, the other a music system □ **www.staahl.com**

4 Coffee table in oak. Similar designs include George (2001) and Solo (1999) by Antonio Citterio □ **www.bebitalia.it**

5 Charles sofa with soft taupe upholstery (1998) by Antonio Citterio □ **www.bebitalia.it**

6 Solid oak parquet flooring □ **for wood flooring, including parquet, see the Directory of Suppliers on pages 152–55**

OCCASIONAL CHAIRS

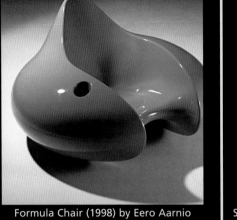

Formula Chair (1998) by Eero Aarnio
□ **www.adelta.de**

Sacco (1968) by Piero Gatti, Cesare Paolini &
Franco Teodoro □ **www.zanotta.it**

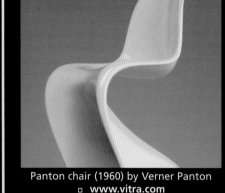

Panton chair (1960) by Verner Panton
□ **www.vitra.com**

Dodo by Mårten Claesson, Eero Koivisto
& Ola Rune □ **www.eandy.com**

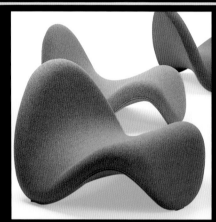

Model No. 577, Tongue (1967) by
Pierre Paulin □ **www.artifort.com**

Bubble Chair (1968) by Eero Aarnio
□ **www.adelta.de**

Wiggle (1972) by Frank O. Gehry
□ **www.vitra.com**

Ball Chair (1966) by Eero Aarnio
□ **www.adelta.de**

S-chair (1988) by Tom Dixon
□ **www.cappellini.it**

Canadian Hard Maple kitchen system
□ **www.poggenpohl.de**

Fiberglass chair (1948–50), Charles & Ray Eames, reissued as Plastic Chair □ **www.vitra.com**

hm26 sofa in brown leather, Fred Scott
□ **www.hitchmylius.co.uk**

Modern classic
by David Bishop at Bluebottle
www.bluebottle.co.uk

In this conversion of a late-nineteenth-century brick-built factory, the open-plan layout makes an ideal space for supper and parties with friends. The architect stripped out the space to create an empty shell and then inserted a minimalist interior, which retains the great sense of space. The owner is a fan of postwar design classics and has spent years scouring markets, auction rooms, and secondhand stores to find his impressive collection of 1950s, '60s, and '70s furniture, lighting, glassware, ceramics, and sculpture.

1 An entire wall of built-in cabinets was designed by the architect to hide the services, provide a huge amount of storage space, and enable the rest of the open-plan room to remain uncluttered. The cabinets are just 12 inches deep, and sheer doors without handles reduce their visual impact on the room □ **www.bluebottle.co.uk**

2 This lamp was discovered in a secondhand store. A French design from the 1960s, it's called Sputnik □ **for vintage furniture and home accessories, see the Directory of Suppliers on pages 152–55**

3 Wooden abstract sculpture by British artist Brian Willsher
□ **www.geocities.com/brianwillsher**

4 The bar stools are a secondhand find; they have been reupholstered in a cream fabric. The style is similar to the Polo bar stool by Robin Day, based on his classic Polo chair (1973) □ **www.loftonline.net**

5 Oversized table made from 13-foot-long scaffolding boards, which were sanded and then stained a dark teak color to match the floor
□ **for architectural salvage and recycled timber, see the Directory of Suppliers on pages 152–55**

6 Reclaimed teak floorboards from an old university building, sanded and finished with Danish oil, which seeps into the surface and hardens to leave a matte surface □ **www.liberon.com**

7 Another secondhand find, the lounge chairs have molded plywood shells standing on a stem foot. They are similar in shape to armchair Model No. 545, Tulip (1965) by Pierre Paulin □ **www.artifort.com**

8 Woolen shagpile rug completes the 1960s look of this great interior. For the ultimate in softness, look for sheepskin rugs
□ **www.boconcept.com**

Model No. PK61 (1955) by Poul Kjærholm
□ **www.fritzhansen.com**

Model No. E1027, Adjustable Table (1927)
by Eileen Gray □ **www.classicon.com**

Lift-Up by Mårten Claesson, Eero Koivisto
& Ola Rune □ **www.nola.se**

Isokon Nesting Tables (1936) by
Marcel Breuer □ **www.isokonplus.com**

Model No. 780/783 (1966) by
Gianfranco Frattini □ **www.cassina.it**

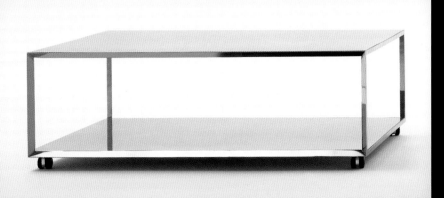

Ministeel Carrello by Carlo Colombo
□ **www.cappellini.it**

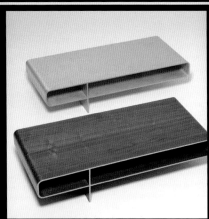

Loop (1996) by Barber Osgerby
□ **www.isokonplus.com**

Kite (2003) by Andreas Weber
□ **www.desalto.it**

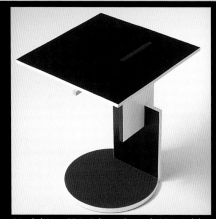

Model No. 634, Schroeder 1 (1922–23) by
Gerrit Thomas Rietveld □ **www.cassina.it**

Tolomeo floor lamp in aluminum (1987), Michele de Lucchi & Giancarlo Fassina □ www.artemide.com

Lounge Chair No. 670 & Ottoman No. 671 in black leather (1956), Charles & Ray Eames □ www.vitra.com

Tulip small side table with white marble tabletop (1956), Eero Saarinen □ www.knollint.com

Rich comfort
by Pablo Uribe

www.studiouribe.com

The refurbishment of this nineteenth-century urban apartment was designed to create a sense of warm modernity. Period details, including the windows, with their pretty colored glass panels, and the cast-iron fireplace, were saved and restored, and then the new finishes carefully installed. Walls are a soft khaki color, and the floor is a rich merbau wood. Into the space a mixture of classic and contemporary furniture has been introduced to give an uncluttered modern, yet homely look.

1 Custom-made lighting designed by Peter Nelson for SKK □ www.skk.net

2 Modular metal wall-fixed shelving system □ www.fontanaarte.it

3 Art Nouveau-style, cast-iron original fireplace, which has been cleaned up and given a matte black finish □ **for architectural salvage, including fireplaces, see the Directory of Suppliers on pages 152–55**

4 Costanza table lamp (1985) by Paolo Rizzatto. Available as floor, table, and pendant lamps, as well as wall lights, with a square natural aluminum stand, which is also available painted black or iron gray. The lamp features a dimmer rod close to the light, which only has to be touched to adjust its brightness. The silk-screen printed polycarbonate shade is available in a range of colors □ www.luceplan.com

5 Apta Collection bench table by Antonio Citterio. Shown in wenge wood on stainless steel frame □ www.maxalto.it

6 A vintage find, this much-sought-after ebonized credenza is by Florence Knoll from 1961 □ **for vintage furniture, see the Directory of Suppliers on pages 152–55** □ Now part of the Florence Knoll Executive Collection, the credenza is still in production under the brand of Knoll Studio □ www.knoll.com

7 Richly colored merbau hardwood floor gives a warm tone to the room. This was bought as a prefinished system floor, with 3/16-inch depth of veneer protected with six coats of lacquer □ **for wood flooring, see the Directory of Suppliers on pages 152–55**

8 Charles sofa in dark gray upholstery (1998) by Antonio Citterio. Shown with Charles bench in lighter gray fabric □ www.bebitalia.it

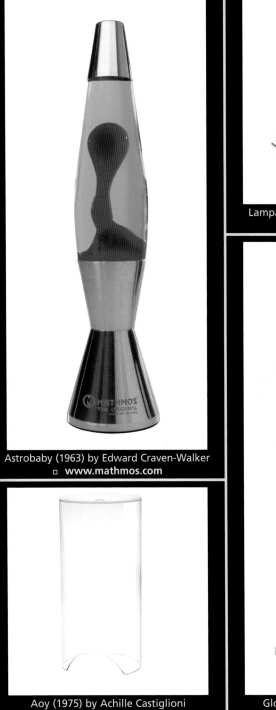

Astrobaby (1963) by Edward Craven-Walker
□ **www.mathmos.com**

Lampadina (1972) by Achille Castiglioni
□ **www.flos.net**

Miss Sissi (1991) by Philippe Starck
□ **www.flos.net**

Aoy (1975) by Achille Castiglioni
□ **www.flos.net**

Glo-ball (1998) by Jasper Morrison
□ **www.flos.net**

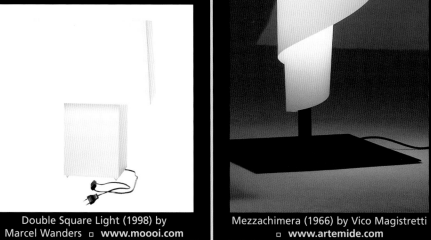

Double Square Light (1998) by
Marcel Wanders □ **www.moooi.com**

Mezzachimera (1966) by Vico Magistretti
□ **www.artemide.com**

Tulip dining table and chairs (1956),
Eero Saarinen □ www.knollint.com

Panthella table lamp in white acrylic (1970),
Verner Panton □ www.louis-poulsen.com

Living It Up
by A-EM Architects
www.a-em.com

This steel, timber, and glass structure demonstrates the potential of underused city rooftops to create contemporary homes. The apartment, with its city-wide views, sits above an undistinguished low-rise appartment block of the 1970s. Access to the space was created by fitting a stair where there had been a closet in the floor below. The highly desirable apartment has floor-to-ceiling walls of glass wrapping around the open-plan living space. Doors slide open for access to the roof terrace. The owners have fitted blinds only to the more enclosed bedrooms, and from the living space they enjoy the ever-changing cityscape.

1 Glo-ball pendant lamp (1998) by Jasper Morrison. A series of floor, table, and pendant lamps, which give a warm ambient light. The floor and table lamps stand on slender stem with large circular bases □ www.flos.net

2 Monkey children's toy (1951) by Kay Bojesen □ www.rosendahl.com

3 Custom-made shelving designed by the architect, using easily available brackets to hold glass shelving □ www.a-em.com

4 An unusual, custom-made fireplace designed by the architect. Ceiling-suspended fireplaces in contemporary interiors are extremely eye-catching □ www.a-em.com

5 A classic glass coffee table is a good choice for such a glassy structure; it is functional and yet doesn't appear to fill up the space. A glass two-tier table can be found in the series designed by Terence Woodgate for SCP □ www.scp.co.uk □ there's also the Sanzeno table (1995) by Emaf Progetti □ www.zanotta.it

6 Freetime sofa (1999) by Antonio Citterio. Forms part of a versatile seating system. The design comprises a bright chrome, tubular metal frame with upholstered cushions sitting on a choice of white, blue, or black belting, which gives a distinctive look and is ecologically sound. The system includes sofas and armchairs, with double upholstering for the backrest and seat, and corner units with adjustable backrest and with or without relax movement □ www.bebitalia.it

Pierre ou Paul (1996) by Ingo Maurer
▫ **www.ingo-maurer.com**

Artichoke (1958) by Poul Henningsen
▫ **www.louis-poulsen.com**

Taraxacum 88 (1988) by Achille Castiglioni
▫ **www.flos.net**

Glo-ball (1998) by Jasper Morrison
▫ **www.flos.net**

Satellite by Vilhelm Wohlert
▫ **www.louis-poulsen.com**

Egg chair (1957) in wicker, suspended on a nickel-plated chain, Nanna & Jørgen Ditzel □ **www.bonacinapierantonio.it**

Jack Light floorlamp (1996), Tom Dixon □ **www.eurolounge.co.uk**

Urban aerie
by Featherstone Associates
www.featherstone-associates.co.uk

This laid-back living space, complete with sunken seating area, sits at the very top of an extremely unusual courtyard house. In a restricted urban site, the architect has succeeded in creating an intriguing home that starts at street level with a modest door set in a blank brick wall. Inside, the stairway climbs to one side of an open courtyard. Sleeping and bathing areas occupy the lower parts of the building, and as the stairway climbs, more light is drawn into the rooms. At the top, the space explodes open into a large kitchen and dining room with steps up to this living space. Another short flight of stairs leads to a rooftop terrace with spectacular city views.

1 Porcelain pendant lamps hung in profusion were from ProtoUK, a company that no longer exists. For more ideas for pendant fixtures visit Tecnolumen □ **www.tecnolumen.de** □ Luceplan □ **www.luceplan.com** □ and Foscarini □ **www.foscarini.com**

2 Brightly colored, upholstered chairs, bought secondhand in a local street market. Among companies making soft sculptural upholstered chairs are Edra □ **www.edra.com** □ Arflex □ **www.arflex.com** □ and ClassiCon □ **www.classicon.com**

3 Sunken seating area. A soft, upholstered seating pit is the perfect place to chill out. Light from the window and rooflight is diffused by the muslin curtain □ **for fabrics, see the Directory of Suppliers on pages 152–55**

4 Seating Pad in blue foam by Michael Young □ **www.cappellini.it**

5 Peran Rustik Glamour pebble flooring in white by Perstorp □ **www.peran.com**

6 Wood flooring in elm, along with other joinery in the house, was completed by Dominic Ash □ **www.dominicash.co.uk**

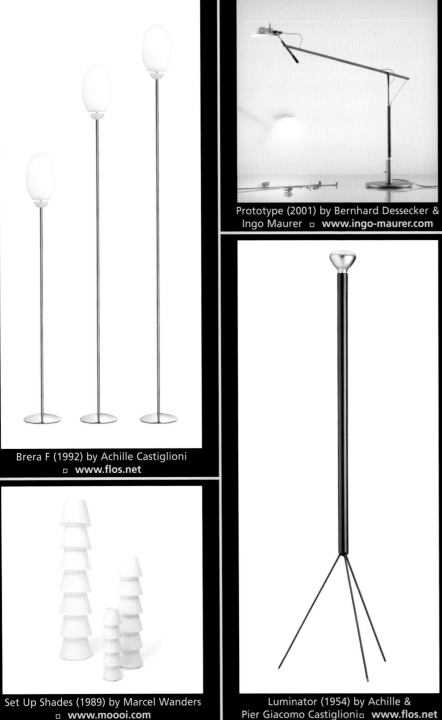

Brera F (1992) by Achille Castiglioni
□ **www.flos.net**

Prototype (2001) by Bernhard Dessecker &
Ingo Maurer □ **www.ingo-maurer.com**

Clitunno (1963) by Vico Magistretti
□ **www.artemide.com**

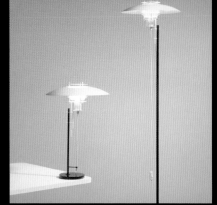

Floorlamp JL2L (1997) by Juha Leiviskä
□ **www.artek.fi**

Set Up Shades (1989) by Marcel Wanders
□ **www.moooi.com**

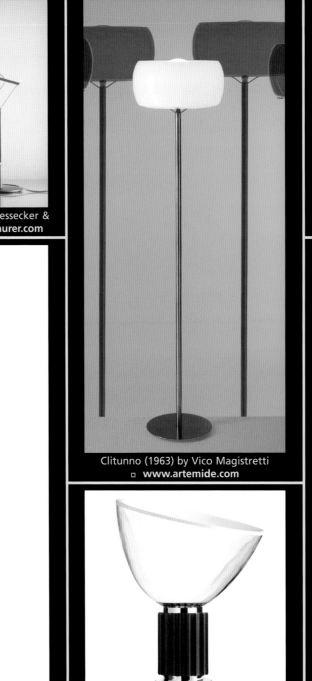

Luminator (1954) by Achille &
Pier Giacomo Castiglioni □ **www.flos.net**

Taccia (1962) by Achille &
Pier Giacomo Castiglioni □ **www.flos.net**

AJ (1957–60) by Arne Jacobsen
□ **www.louis-poulsen.com**

Arco floorlamp with marble base (1962),
Achille & Pier Giacomo Castiglioni □ **www.flos.net**

Costanza adjustable floorlamp (1985),
Paolo Rizzatto □ **www.luceplan.com**

Urban living

by Fiona Mclean at Mclean Quinlan

www.mcleanquinlan.com

The owner of this protected historic townhouse enjoys the contrast of old and new. The eighteenth-century building retains many original details, including window shutters and ceiling moldings, which have been painted white to form a neutral backdrop to the contemporary interior. The muted grays are given an exciting boost by the red bench.

1 Custom-made gray Acero limestone fire surround, in a contemporary style to complement the interior □ **for fires, stoves, and fireplaces, see the Directory of Suppliers on pages 152–55**

2 SFS 03 digital television with 29½"flat screen □ **www.panasonic.com**

3 Slender slatted birch blinds, which have been fitted to filter and soften the powerful afternoon sun in this west-facing room □ **for blinds, see the Directory of Suppliers on pages 152–55**

4 Charles sofa in gray imitation suede (1998) by Antonio Citterio □ **www.bebitalia.it** □ upholstered in Glove □ **www.kvadrat.dk**

5 Charles bench in red wool (1998) by Antonio Citterio □ **www.bebitalia.it** □ upholstered in Scarlet □ **www.butefabrics.com**

6 Fra table with white lacquered table top by Roberto Barbieri. The frame is flat steel, available in black, graphite, or nickeled varnish □ **www.bebitalia.it**

7 Gray linen and wool blend flatweave rug, which complements the gray of the sofa and anchors the room □ **www.kasthall.se**

8 Solid oak flooring, which has been finished in a subtle matte varnish to provide the room with a warm color base □ **for wood flooring, see the Directory of Suppliers on pages 152–55**

• The dining table is a key item of furniture—dark wood and antique pieces have a more formal feel than pale wood and contemporary styles.

• Comfortable dining chairs are a must, unless you want guests to leave early—choose a design that combines comfortable seats with a shaped backrest for good support.

• For a formal style, use rich, dark colors; for informality choose lighter, fresher colors.

• Storage space close to the table is extremely useful. A sideboard or dresser is ideal for serving bowls, place mats, glasses, candles, linen, and even flatware and dishes.

• Dimmer controls on the lighting make it easy to switch from bright, upbeat moods to a quieter, more restful atmosphere.

• Candles may be a cliché, but they do provide a calming, flattering, and romantic light.

In most homes the dining room is an endangered space; separate dining rooms are often converted into home offices or combined with the living room. Despite our increasingly informal attitude to mealtimes, most homes retain a dining table, which becomes the focus for entertaining; and there remain plenty of occasions of the space—a polished, dark-wood, antique piece of furniture has a more formal feel to it than a light oak refectory table. Chairs need to be chosen carefully, too. To save space, stacking and folding chairs are a good idea, but comfort should always be a priority, especially if you enjoy people sitting around the table talking for

DINING ROOMS

when sharing food with friends and family is a thoroughly enjoyable way to pass the time. In an open-plan space, the ideal table should complement any existing furnishings. Where space is limited, it may need to be a design that folds up and stows away. In a designated dining room, the choice of table is key to the character hours. Lighting certainly helps to set the mood. Bright light levels are fine for children's parties. But they can be uncomfortable for grown-up suppers, so dimmer switches are useful. A pendant lamp over the table helps to make the plates and glasses sparkle, and candles always cast a restful, flattering, and romantic light

Double Decker (2001) by Marcel Wanders
□ **www.moooi.com**

Strata by Edward Carpenter & Rushton Bros.
□ **www.timeframe.info**

Table 81B (1933–35) by Alvar Aalto
□ **www.artek.fi**

Arc by Mårten Claesson, Eero Koivisto & Ola Rune
□ **www.asplund.org**

Dining Table 746 (1941) by Jens Risom
□ **www.knoll.com**

Level Table by Peter Emrys-Roberts
□ **www.driade.com**

Model No. 2650, Leonardo (1950) by Achille Castiglioni
□ **www.zanotta.it**

Lem barstool in white leather (2000),
Shin & Tomoko Azumi □ www.lapalma.it

Rondo chair in white laminate,
Erik Jørgensen □ www.danerka.dk

Minimal Dining Table in walnut, De La Espada
□ www.delaespada.com

Polished finish
by Denton Corker Marshall Architects

www.dcm-group.com

Glass, cedar, zinc, and concrete have been combined to create this contemporary home and studio with roof garden on a small urban plot, previously occupied by old stables and overlooking a park. Designed for an Australian photographer and his art director wife in London, the living space floats above the entire first-floor studio. At its heart is a spacious dining, cooking, and living area, where the architect has played with blurring the boundaries between inside and out by building in huge sliding doors, which open up one corner entirely to make the room feel like an open terrace.

1 Custom-made kitchen system designed by the architect. The sheer, white-lacquered doors are push release. The island unit features an inset panel of walnut veneer, which links to the walnut dining table □ **www.dcm-group.com**

2 Raised up on a concrete plinth to maximize its effect as focal point of the space, this custom-made hearth houses a contemporary gas fireplaces. The special heat-tolerant stones are made to resemble pebbles □ **www.realflame.co.uk**

3 Gorki collection sofa (2002) in purple fabric upholstery by Rodolfo Dordoni. Collection includes a coordinating bench. Available in fabric upholstery or leather □ **www.minotti.it**

4 An antique find, the stainless-steel, glass, and wood coffee table by Merrow Associates is probably from the 1970s □ **for vintage furniture, see the Directory of Suppliers on pages 152–55**

5 Geometric lamp with decorative shade, from Maisonette, which complements the vintage coffee table □ **www.maisonette.uk.com**

6 The surface of the structural concrete floor has been painstakingly ground to produce this amazing polished finish □ **for concrete flooring, see the Directory of Suppliers on pages 152–55**

Cherner Chair (1958) by Paul Goldman
□ **www.chernerchair.com**

Butterfly Chair (1958) by Lucian R. Ercolani
□ **www.ercol.com**

Model No. 699, Superleggera by
Gio Ponti □ **www.cassina.it**

LCM (1945) by Charles & Ray Eames
□ **www.vitra.com**

DCM (1945) by Charles & Ray Eames
□ **www.vitra.com**

T-0507N Chair (1954) by Tadaomi Mizunoe
□ **www.tendo-mokko.co.jp**

Pop by Eero Koivisto
□ **www.offecct.se**

Model No. 214 (1859) by Michael Thonet
□ **www.thonet.de**

S-7260B Chair (1955) by Charlotte Perriand
□ **www.tendo-mokko.co.jp**

Bend by Mårten Claesson
□ **www.swedese.se**

Dining feast

by Claesson Koivisto Rune

www.claesson-koivisto-rune.se

In a dramatic bid to open up this large apartment, walls were torn down to transform the place from seven rooms to just three main free-flowing spaces for sitting, cooking and eating, and sleeping. This handsome home, once the Soviet ambassador's residence in Stockholm, is on the fourth floor of a 1920s downtown building. It has windows on three sides and is blessed with generous sunlight. The preparatory work entailed removing walls and stripping out some of the old interior, but the architects left in place much of the original plaster moldings and decorative architraving "so that the new additions could be seen in clear contrast with the backdrop of the old." Walls were painted white, and, where damaged, the oak flooring was restored and then given a white-limed finish. In such large spaces, rugs can be used effectively to define different areas.

1 Custom-made dining table designed by the architects, Mårten Claesson, Eero Koivisto, and Ola Rune. This monumental table was made from a single African walnut tree trunk. Measuring 14¾ feet in length, it had to be craned into the fourth-floor apartment through a window □ **www.claesson-koivisto-rune.se**

2 Smith, a flat bowl or fruit plate, by Eero Koivisto □ **www.david.se**

3 Line rug in natural and brown by Ritva Puotila. This is one of a basic collection of 56 designs created out of the harmonious combinations of six patterns and 11 color alternatives. Unusually, the rug is made using 86 percent woven paper yarn and 14 percent cotton □ **www.woodnotes.fi**

4 Original oak parquet flooring □ **for wood flooring, including parquet, see the Directory of Suppliers on pages 152–55** □ The parquet flooring has been cleaned, restored, and then finished with a white stain □ **www.triptrap.com**

5 Lines rug by Alfredo Häberli. An intriguing carpet in 100 percent New Zealand wool. The textured finish is reminiscent of a plowed field or rock worn by rivulets of water □ **www.asplund.org**

6 Metro sofa (1999) by Piero Lissoni. Upholstered in gray-blue fabric □ **www.livingdivani.it**

Bolla floorlamp (1999), Michael Sodeau □ **www.gervasoni1882.com**

Y-chair (1950), also known as the Wishbone chair, Hans J. Wegner □ **www.carlhansen.com**

Model No. 2532, Marcuso (1969) by Marco Zanuso
□ **www.zanotta.it**

Model No. CH008 (1954) by Hans J. Wegner
□ **www.carlhansen.com**

City by Mårten Claesson, Eero Koivisto & Ola Rune
□ **www.irenuffici.com**

Model No. 322, D.S.1 (1918) by Charles Rennie Mackintosh
□ **www.cassina.it**

Model No. P970, Plano by Pelikan Design
□ **www.fritzhansen.com**

Model No. 1312, Dining Table (1966) by Warren Platner
□ **www.knollint.com**

S chair (1988) with woven rush seat, Tom Dixon □ **www.cappellini.it**

LIM dining table with frosted safety glass tabletop, Bruno Fattorini/Studio MDF □ **www.mdfitalia.it**

The Classic radiator, Bisque □ **www.bisque.co.uk**

JIM dining chairs (1999) with red upholstery, Gijs Papavoine □ **www.montis.nl**

Monumental scale

by David Mikhail Architects

www.davidmikhail.com

This airy dining and kitchen area was created during the refurbishment and extension of a registered landmark townhouse. The architect's clever space engineering involved dropping the level of the floor into what had been a dark basement to produce an extremely tall room with direct access to the garden. To emphasize the monumental feel of the space, a huge, 13-feet-tall sliding cedar door now leads to the outside terrace. Additional top light enters the kitchen through a silicon-jointed glass box, which has been added to the roof.

1 Custom-made geometric, built-in wall cabinet system designed by the architect □ **www.davidmikhail.com**

2 Filo pendant lamp (1994) by Peter Christian. The polycarbonate shade, shown here in orange, is available in a range of colors □ **www.aktiva.co.uk**

3 Aluminum pendant lamp. Similar pendant lamps are available from Ikea □ **www.ikea.com**

4 Architectural glass roof with silicon joints □ **for architectural glass, see the Directory of Suppliers on pages 152–55**

5 Kitchen units designed by the architect □ **www.davidmikhail.com** □ Made by adapting a basic Ikea system, then finished in white and gray □ **www.ikea.com**

6 Custom-made stainless-steel worktop and backsplash □ **for kitchen furniture, see the Directory of Suppliers on pages 152–55**

7 D line range by Knud Holscher. This range of handles first appeared in the 1970s, but continues to be developed. Available in satin stainless steel □ **www.dline.com**

8 Solid ash floor planks with a 2mm (⅛") v-joint specified by the architect, which gives the floor subtle visual interest □ **for wood flooring, see the Directory of Suppliers on pages 152–55**

9 Oversized, 13-feet-tall sliding door to the garden, designed by the architect □ **www.davidmikhail.com** □ Constructed in cedar. Top hung using sliding gear by Geze □ **www.geze.de**

Cornflake by Mårten Claesson, Eero Koivisto
& Ola Rune □ **www.offecct.se**

Polo Chair (1973) by Robin Day
□ **www.loftonline.net**

Model No. PK9, Tulip Chair (1960) by
Poul Kjærholm □ **www.fritzhansen.com**

Doppio by Eero Koivisto
□ **www.offecct.se**

Hudson (2000) by Philippe Starck
□ **www.emeco.net**

Model No. 3107, Series 7 (1955) by
Arne Jacobsen □ **www.fritzhansen.com**

Afternoon (2001) by Eero Koivisto
□ **www.skandiform.se**

T-3047M Ply Chair (1960) by Saburo Inui
□ **www.tendo-mokko.co.jp**

Model No. 1296, Side Chair (1950–52) by
Harry Bertoia □ **www.knollint.com**

Model No. VM101 VicoDuo (1997) by
Vico Magistretti □ **www.fritzhansen.com**

Tulip pedestal dining table with polished white marble tabletop (1956), Eero Saarinen □ **www.knollint.com**

Series 7 chairs (1955) with white laminate seats, Arne Jacobsen □ **www.fritzhansen.com**

Bombo bar stools (1997) with white ABS plastic seats, Stefano Giovannoni □ **www.magisdesign.com**

White Penthouse
by John Crummay & Robin Rout

www.johncrummay.com □ www.robinrout.com

The designers of this apartment bought the rights to build on the roof of a converted nineteenth-century warehouse apartment. They then constructed a steel and glass rectangular box with a continuous band of horizontal windows, which provides a 360-degree view of the cityscape. The pristine white interior was created to provide an area of calm to contrast with the busy city outside.

1 Lighting throughout is mostly 30mm (1⅜") ceiling-recessed low-voltage halogen downlighters from the Concord range of Sylvania □ **www.syvlania-lighting.com** □ The system is computer controlled to provide a range of mood settings □ **www.lutron.com**

2 Radar armchairs and ottomans in white fabric upholstery by James Irvine □ **www.bebitalia.it**

3 High-backed oak chairs designed by Robert Williams from Pearl Dot □ e-mail: enq@pearldot.com

4 Lunar sofa in white fabric upholstery by James Irvine □ **www.bebitalia.it**

5 To complement the industrial aesthetic of the Bulthaup kitchen □ **www.bulthaup.com** □ a metalworking firm was commissioned to wrap the chunky breakfast bar in stainless steel □ **for kitchen furniture, see the Directory of Suppliers on pages 152–55**

6 The high-gloss white flooring looks like wooden planks but is, in fact, custom-made using fire-retardant and moisture-resistant MDF with beveled edges. The tough, glossy white coating was spray finished for a smooth sheen, using specialist floor paint from the International range □ **www.akzonobel.com**

Model No. 451, La Basilica (1977) by Mario Bellini
□ www.cassina.it

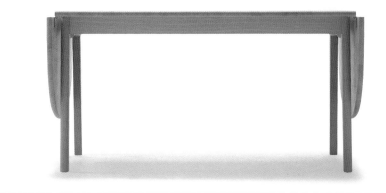

Model No. CH006 (1982) by Hans J. Wegner
□ www.carlhansen.com

Bend by Mårten Claesson, Eero Koivisto & Ola Rune
□ www.swedese.se

Table Y805A (1946–47) by Alvar Aalto
□ www.artek.fi

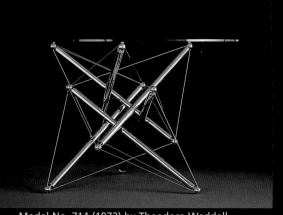

Model No. 714 (1973) by Theodore Waddell
□ www.cassina.it

Space engineers
by Plastik Architects
www.plastik-architects.net

One of the architect's most impressive skills is space engineering, which was certainly put to good use in this modest-size Victorian row house, which was refurbished and opened up for its current owners. Because the budget for the refurbishment works was fairly restrained, the remodeling had to be subtle, yet effective. The first floor had comprised two small rooms; to open them up and connect them visually the architect opened up a former window to the ground, to mirror the doorway in the separating wall. The dining space now benefits from extra natural lighting entering through the glassy kitchen extension beyond. Floor-to-ceiling shelves provide valuable storage for the owner's impressive book collection. The choice of a glass-topped table ensures that light flow and views are uninterrupted through the space, which helps to make it feel larger, and the circular shape is a well-chosen, space-efficient design. White chairs help to keep the space bright and airy.

1 Ceiling-recessed lights are often chosen for small spaces instead of pendant lights, because they provide good-quality, sparkling light and don't distract the eye ▫ **for lighting, see the Directory of Suppliers on pages 152–55**

2 Floor-to-ceiling shelving is the most space-efficient type and provides room for displaying objects together with storing books. Designed by the architect and made on site by the building contractor. By being painted white, the same color as the wall, the shelves recede visually ▫ **www.plastik-architects.net**

3 The sheer finish of the oak floor also helps to make the space look and feel streamlined ▫ **for wood flooring, see the Directory of Suppliers on pages 152–55**

4 A cowhide rug, sourced by the client, adds extra texture and pattern to the room ▫ **for carpets and rugs, see the Directory of Suppliers on pages 152–55**

Vintage dining table; for similar, see La Rotonda (1976), Mario Bellini ▫ **www.cassina.it**

Rondo chair in white laminated plywood, Erik Jørgensen ▫ **www.danerka.dk**

Model No. 150, Tulip Chair (1956) by
Eero Saarinen □ **www.knollint.com**

Model No. 100, Follia (1934) by
Giuseppe Terragni □ **www.zanotta.it**

Model No. 413, CAB (1977) by
Mario Bellini □ **www.cassina.it**

Model No. S32 (1929–30) by
Marcel Breuer □ **www.thonet.de**

Model No. S664 by Eddie Harlis
□ **www.thonet.de**

Classica (1996) by Piero Lissoni
□ **www.cappellini.it**

Model No. 3101, Ant Chair (1952) by
Arne Jacobsen □ **www.fritzhansen.com**

Model No. 2015, Viola (1997) by
Tamar Ben David □ **www.zanotta.it**

Model No. 2090, Tonietta (1985) by
Enzo Mari □ **www.zanotta.it**

Fucsia 3 pendant lamp (1996),
Achille Castiglioni □ **www.flos.net**

DCM (Dining Chair Metal) in black plywood (1945),
Charles & Ray Eames □ **www.vitra.com**

Make-to-order dining

by Featherstone Associates & Dominic Ash

www.featherstone-associates.co.uk □

www.dominicash.co.uk

Forming part of a converted office building, this apartment was bought by the owners during the conversion works. Their early purchase enabled them to organize the spaces exactly as they wanted for their young family. With the help of the architect, they achieved three bedrooms, instead of the two planned by the developer, and oriented the living space to the southwest, in order to overlook the local park. They also obtained a permit to build in additional windows, which flood the interior with natural sunlight. Much of the furniture, using a variety of different woods, has been designed and made by one of the owners, furniture maker Dominic Ash.

1 Wall of kitchen units by Dominic Ash. Built using beech veneer with glossy spray-painted white doors. The doors incorporate a neat indented finger-pull detail to avoid the use of handles, which would spoil the sheer finish. The white of the units helps them to meld into the white of the wall □ **for furniture designers and makers, see the Directory of Suppliers on pages 152–55**

2 Mosaic mirror tiles, readily available in most home centers, add sparkle □ **for tiles, see the Directory of Suppliers on pages 152–55**

3 American black walnut was selected as the material for the island, also by Dominic Ash. It was chosen for its warmth and as a contrast to the white of the cabinets. The island houses the oven, cooktop, a set of drawers, and a trash can. To bring out the grain, and for a lustrous finish, the wood is finished with a natural oil, as is the table and the bench unit □ **for furniture designers and makers, see the Directory of Suppliers on pages 152–55**

4 Dining table designed by Dominic Ash and made in rich-colored wenge wood □ **for furniture designers and makers, see the Directory of Suppliers on pages 152–55**

5 The bench, designed and made by Dominic Ash, is in American black walnut and provides storage for CDs, DVDs, and videos □ **for furniture designers and makers, see the Directory of Suppliers on pages 152–55**

6 The ash floor is laid over infloor heating; it is given an oiled finish □ **for wood flooring, see the Directory of Suppliers on pages 152–55**

Unit by Mårten Claesson, Eero Koivisto & Ola Rune
□ **www.asplund.org**

Model No. 750, Florence (1999) by Alfredo Häberli
□ **www.zanotta.it**

C5 by Bo Steenberg
□ **www.opus1living.com**

Segno by Carlo Colombo
□ **www.cappellini.it**

Wing (1999) by Michael Sodeau
□ **www.isokonplus.com**

Model No. SB02, Farah by Philipp Marinzer
□ **www.e15.com**

PH 3/2 table lamps (1926), Poul Henningsen □ **www.louis-poulsen.com**

Antique sideboard clad in stainless steel, Tony Heine □ **www.heinedesign.com**

Barcelona chair (1929) in black leather, Ludwig Mies van der Rohe □ **www.knoll.com**

Antique Chic
by Heine Design

www.heinedesign.com

This former bakery in the heart of Copenhagen was gutted, walls were torn down, and the whole space was reinvented as an open-plan apartment by its owner, furniture designer Tony Heine. The interior is used to show off some of Heine's more unusual creations, such as the antique-and-modern dining table.

1 Triax pendant lamp □ **www.herstal.dk**

2 KV6 two-handled faucet (1969) by Arne Jacobsen □ **www.vola.com**

3 Custom-made kitchen units designed by the owner. The small white island unit has a stainless steel top □ **www.heinedesign.com**

4 A metal shelving unit on wheels from the industrial ranges designed for kitchens, laboratories, factories, etc., by shelving and storage expert Metro □ **www.metro.com**

5 The humidor in cherry wood and antique cut-glass decanters are all antique-shop finds □ **for vintage furniture and home accessories, see the Directory of Suppliers on pages 152–55**

6 These sensuously curved legs originally belonged to an antique oak table. Because the tabletop was split and impossible to repair, Heine kept just the legs and incorporated them into a new steel-framed table with a 5mm- (¼") glass top □ **www.heinedesign.com**

7 The provenance of these black and aluminum chairs is uncertain; however, they bear a strong resemblance to some classic designs that remain in production, including Polo Chair (1977) by Robin Day □ **www.loftonline.net** and Box Chair (1975–6) by Enzo Mari □ **www.driade.com**

8 The original solid oak floor has been finished with an opaque white varnish □ **for wood flooring, see the Directory of Suppliers on pages 152–55**

9 Brown leather-covered ottoman with stainless steel legs by Heine Design □ **www.heinedesign.com**

Fucsia 8 (1996) by Achille Castiglioni
□ **www.flos.net**

HMB 25 (1925) by Marianne Brandt &
Hans Przyrembel □ **www.tecnolumen.com**

Zettel'z (1997) by Ingo Maurer
□ **www.ingo-maurer.com**

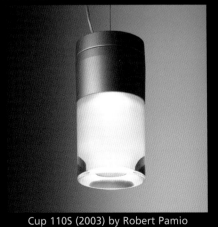

Cup 110S (2003) by Robert Pamio
□ **www.iguzzini.com**

Square Boon (2002) by Piet Boon
□ **www.moooi.com**

Toldbod (2001) by Louis Poulsen Lighting
□ **www.louis-poulsen.com**

Romeo Moon S2 (1996) by Philippe Starck
□ **www.flos.net**

Danish design pendant lamp; for similar see
□ **www.louis-poulsen.com** or **www.flos.net**

Alvar Aalto Collection vase (1936),
Alvar Aalto □ **www.iittala.com**

Room to breathe
by Wahlström and Steijner Architects
www.wahlstrom-steijner.se

The architect's concept for this house was to combine light, space, and ecology. Close to the shore, the contemporary-style frame house has been designed to maximize the great sea views, and includes a sundeck on the roof for a panoramic view of the Gothenburg Archipelago, Sweden. Inside, the first floor is a private zone with bedrooms, bathroom, and laundry, while upstairs is this large, open living space with sea views. The house incorporates numerous ecological features including healthy insulation materials and low-odor paint.

1 Piu Avantgarde, a circular stove finished in stainless steel and with a 180-degree glass firedoor □ **www.spartherm.com**

2 Basic/Original sofa, designed by Ire Design Group, made by Ire Mobel □ **www.iremobel.se**

3 Ride-on rocking horse, made by the late Arne Karlsson. A similar rocking horse is also part of the range of classics by Playsam □ **www.playsam.com**

4 Blond wood dining table, bought in Italy. A table with chamfered top and retro-style splayed legs has been designed by Matthew Hilton for SCP. Called Thin, it is made in American walnut with a glass inset top □ **www.scp.co.uk**

5 A wool rug in a neutral stone color with a pattern of raised circles □ **www.ikea.com**

6 Italian design, metal frame with woven seat and curved wood back. Bought in Italy. For chairs in a similar style with this curved, embracing backrest, see Roger from Ikea □ **www.ikea.com**

- Choose between a standard kitchen with built-in cabinetry or the eclectic style with separate pieces of furniture.

- The character of the space will be created by the kitchen cabinets—sheer laminate doors have a sleek look and are easy to keep clean; wood is softer and more family friendly.

- So many appliances are temptingly beautiful; choose only what you need, and resist being seduced by gadgetry.

- Task lighting is essential to safe working—lights should be fitted under wall-fixed cabinets or on the wall, so that you avoid working in your own shadow.

- The design of kitchen sinks has come a long way in recent years. There are now multi-task sinks with fitted chopping boards, pull-out spray faucets, waste disposals, and more.

- Smart handles make a budget kitchen look a million dollars.

As we all know, the kitchen is the hub of the home and, in most cases, the hardest-working space. When planning a kitchen, the first three considerations are your cooking needs, available space, and size of budget. If you cook frequently, it is worth investing in a hard-working space; for those who cook occasionally, the best advice is to

two. A kitchen's character comes from the cabinets and appliances chosen—the professional style is associated with stainless steel; sheer laminates have an urban look, while natural and painted wood are a softer style. The choice of countertops and flooring underline the choice of cabinet—hard-wearing stainless steel is the choice of chefs;

KITCHENS

opt for a modest scheme. Take care when choosing appliances; it is easy to overspend on unnecessary gadgets. The room size has a major influence on a kitchen layout: the smallest spaces can be highly functional when lined with sleek cabinets. In larger rooms there's the option of built-in cabinetry or separate pieces, or a mixture of the

granite and marble are expensive and chic; laminate is extremely tough and inexpensive; wood is appealing, but usually requires maintenance to keep it looking good. To make the transition from busy breakfasts to smart suppers, good task lighting, combined with flexible and imaginative general lighting, is key.

Case System 5.0 in stainless steel (2000) by Piero Lissoni
□ **www.boffi.com**

Tecna by Studio Kairos
□ **www.varennapoliform.it**

LT (2002) by Piero Lissoni
□ **www.boffi.com**

Gandhara (2001) by Minotti Cucine
□ **www.minotticucine.it**

Case System 5.0 in white Pral (2000) by Piero Lissoni
□ **www.boffi.com**

Tara wall-mounted faucet (1991), Sieger
Design □ **www.dornbracht.com**

Teak veneer slimline kitchen cabinets with inset
stainless splashback □ **www.projectorange.com**

Teak chic
by Project Orange

www.projectorange.com

When the owners took over this nineteenth-century house, it
was in a poor state of repair, but had the potential to become
an interesting family home. The kitchen was particularly basic,
with just an old stone sink and one faucet. The architect has
extended outward with a frameless glass extension to increase
the space by 50 percent and excavated 1⅔ feet for a luxurious
ceiling height. The new extension has achieved the owners'
wish to have more connection with the courtyard, which has
been finished with wooden decking and can be lit at night.

1 An ingenious space-saving feature of the room is this L-shaped
concrete bench seating, which also doubles as part of the structure
for the glass extension □ **www.projectorange.com**

2 Teak dining table designed by the architect to match the
kitchen cabinets □ **www.projectorange.com**

3 Slabs of Acero blue limestone flooring. To ensure that flooring
is properly installed and sealed against staining, always get advice
from the supplier □ **for stone flooring, see the Directory of Suppliers
on pages 152–55**

4 Stainless steel electrical outlet and switch from Wandsworth's Classic
Series 2 □ **www.wandsworth-electrical.com**

K10 (2001) by Norbert Wangen
□ **www.norbert-wangen.com**

SC 60 by SieMatic
□ **www.siematic.de**

Orlando (2001–2002) by Leicht Design Studio
□ **www.leicht.de**

Grafics (2001–2002) by Leicht Design Studio
□ **www.leicht.de**

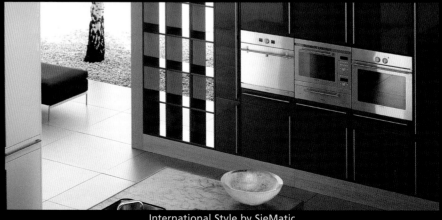

International Style by SieMatic
□ **www.siematic.de**

INXX faucet in stainless steel
□ www.moraarmatur.se

Beach stainless steel kitchen sink
□ www.franke.com

White laminate kitchen cabinets with concealed
handles □ www.rbarchitecture.com

Ice white
by Rahel Belatchew Lerdell
www.rbarchitecture.com

This serene galley-style kitchen sits on the second floor of a contemporary-style frame house, which has been cleverly built on a tricky, north-facing hillside site. Along with the difficulties of the plot, the architect owner and designer of the house also had to work within local regulations that restricted the size and height of the building. From the start, every effort was made to turn these constrictions into an advantage. Bedrooms are placed on the first floor, while the living room and kitchen are above, for optimum light. The horizontal band of windows is designed for enjoying the views and, at the same time, maintain privacy. Echoing the band of windows, a long internal bar counter opening sits between the kitchen and dining areas. Since it is part of the main living area, the architect wanted to integrate the kitchen into the space, so most of the appliances are contained in cabinets. Even the means of opening the cabinets is concealed; there are "handles" carved into the edge of the doors, so they operate without catches or magnets. The only item that couldn't be hidden was the Gaggenau oven.

1 A big trough of light has been built into the ceiling while additional task lighting for the countertop is provided by small fixtures underneath the upper cabinets □ www.rbarchitecture.com

2 A neat and unusual feature is the sound-system speakers, which have been fitted into the ceiling. For a range of speakers and a custom installation service, see BW Speakers □ www.bwspeakers.com

3 Swanstone white countertop. An extremely durable composite material, suitable for kitchens and bathrooms, available in a huge range of colors and textures □ www.swanstone.com

4 Induction cooktop by Bosch □ www.bosch.com

5 Pine boards stained very dark brown with a water-based stain. For ecologically sound wood stain products, see Minwax □ www.minwax.com □ or Behr □ www.behr.com

Extending Table (2004) by Matthew Hilton
◻ **www.scp.co.uk**

AVL Shaker Table (1999) by Joep van Lieshout
◻ www.moooi.com

Model No. CH318 (1960) by Hans J. Wegner
◻ **www.carlhansen.com**

Model No. e6, Dolmen Table by Carlo Colombo
◻ **www.poliform.it**

Thin (2001) by Matthew Hilton
◻ **www.scp.co.uk**

Concrete and resin mix slab tabletop on cinder block supports □ www.icebergarchitecturestudio.com

Ponza dining chair with dark wood finish, Henri Becq □ **www.modenature.com**

Rough, polished, and painted
by Etienne van den Berg

www.icebergarchitecturestudio.com

The industrial aesthetic of this loft conversion has been continued in the kitchen, where concrete—rough, polished, and painted—is the predominant material. Vestiges of the original structure, including the cast-iron columns and vaulted ceiling, are celebrated by being left exposed. Into this rugged interior has been fitted a refined kitchen; cabinets are given sheet zinc doors; and the countertops and dining table are constructed in concrete, blended with resin for a water- and stainproof finish.

1 To tie in with the front of the cabinet doors, the shelves are also made from zinc □ **for metal and metal workers, see the Directory of Suppliers on pages 152–55**

2 Custom-made kitchen island unit, countertop, and dining table, designed by the architect □ **www.icebergarchitecturestudio.com** □ All made using concrete that has been blended with resin for a water- and stainproof finish. The material was mixed and poured on site, then smoothed with a trowel. Once dry, the material was given extra protection with a wax finish □ **for concrete worktops, see the Directory of Suppliers on pages 152–55**

3 All appliances in this kitchen, including the dishwasher and refrigerator, are from Smeg □ **www.smeg.it**

4 Walls painted with wipe-clean, matte-finish chalkboard paint. Available from the International range □ **www.akzonobel.com**

5 Polished concrete floor slabs □ **for concrete flooring, see the Directory of Suppliers on pages 152–55**

Chair 69 (1933–35) by Alvar Aalto
□ **www.artek.fi**

ERO/S (2001) by Philippe Starck
□ **www.kartell.it**

AVL Shaker Chair (1999) by
Joep van Lieshout □ **www.moooi.com**

DC Chair by Tadhg & Simon O'Driscoll
□ **www.oddesign.com**

Trinidad (1993) by Nanna Ditzel
□ **www.fredericia.com**

Model No. e11, Carmel Chair by
Roberto Lazzeroni □ **www.poliform.it**

Model No. 1006, Navy Chair (1940s) by
Emeco □ **www.emeco.net**

Oyster Chair (1998) by Nigel Coates
□ **www.lloydloom.com**

Foto pendant lamp in matte brushed aluminium
□ **www.ikea.com**

Rotaflow kitchen faucet with silk steel finish
from the Classic Studio Range □ **www.franke.com**

Compact Range CPX 652-E stainless steel kitchen sink with silk
steel finish from the Classic Studio Range □ **www.franke.com**

Fiberglass Chair (1948–50), Charles & Ray Eames,
now reissued as Plastic Chair □ **www.vitra.com**

Extreme scheme
by Nick McMahon

email: mail@nickmcmahon.co.uk

The highly unusual and extreme lime green and egg-yolk yellow color scheme for this kitchen happened entirely by mistake—a mix-up with the contractor. However, the owners have grown to like it, so it has been allowed to remain. The apartment is in a converted meat-processing factory, where the thick concrete walls and floors provided a sturdy shell and the perfect insulation for a residential conversion. The kitchen is formed from a horseshoe-shaped arrangement of cabinets with dining area beyond. This is separated from the living area with a wall of glass blocks.

1 Black mosaic tiles are used as a backsplash and given extra interest by the use of white grout □ **for tiles, see the Directory of Suppliers on pages 152–55**

2 Custom-made table with metal trestle-style legs, which features an unusual glass top called Lenscore—a sheet glass sandwich with an aluminum honeycomb center. It is a material that has been developed by the architect and is extremely strong for its light weight □ **e mail: mail@nickmcmahon.co.uk**

3 The horseshoe-shaped kitchen is based on a standard European 600mm (23½") module, but has been custom designed by the architect. It is highly space-efficient, as one wall of cabinets forms a room divider between kitchen and dining areas □ **e-mail: mail@nickmcmahon.co.uk**

4 Beech countertop made from strips of wood. This type of countertop looks great but requires maintenance and care to keep it that way, it doesn't survive well in very damp conditions □ **for wood, including countertops, see the Directory of Suppliers on pages 152–55**

5 The floor is finished in an intriguing end-grain ash, often to be found in industrial flooring, where small tiles of the material are supplied and laid in sheets, like fine parquet □ **for wood flooring, including parquet, see the Directory of Suppliers on pages 152–55** □ The floor is then treated with three coats of matt waterbased sealant □ **www.bona.com**

6 Painting entitled "Mrs. Ballentine and her father with her record salmon" (1992) by Andy Carter

Q Stak (1953) by Robin Day
□ **www.loftonline.net**

La Marie (1999) by Philippe Starck
□ **www.kartell.it**

Model No. 4867, Universale (1965–67) by Joe Colombo
□ **www.kartell.it**

Stacking Chair (1957) by Lucian R. Ercolani
□ **www.ercol.com**

Tate Contract (2000) by Jasper Morrison
□ **www.cappellini.it**

Model No. KS110, Runner (1997) by Kasper Salto
□ **www.fritzhansen.com**

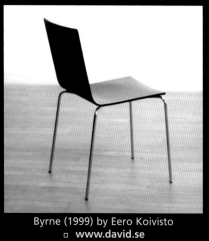

Byrne (1999) by Eero Koivisto
□ **www.david.se**

Attityd kitchen system, Mikael Warnhammar, adapted by the architect □ **www.ikea.com**

La Marie chair in crystal (1999), Philippe Starck □ **www.kartell.it**

1

2

3

4

5

See through
by Tonkin Liu

www.tonkinliu.co.uk

In this conversion of a riverside warehouse, at the lower levels of the building, light was at a premium. To maximize the sense of light, the architect designed a room that is startlingly transparent. Dining chairs are entirely see-through, while the kitchen is almost a mirage. Clever lighting design gives the effect of more natural daylight than is the reality. The use of white and gray in the color scheme helps to reflect light around the space—a device often used in Scandinavian countries, where winter sunlight is in short supply. Accessories in cherry red draw the eye around the room.

1 Custom-made lighting designed by the architect □ **www.tonkinliu.co.uk** □ Above the sink, a long white strip of MDF acts as a baffle for the pair of wall-fixed fluorescent tubes, which sit behind and provide a soft glow □ **www.encapsulite.com**

2 The small window has been made to appear much larger and brighter by setting fluorescent strips in the window recesses. A shade pulled down in front of the artificial light makes it appear to be very sunny outside □ **www.encapsulite.com**

3 Corian countertop. An extremely tough and almost indestructible product, blending natural materials with pure acrylic polymer. It has a silky and luxurious texture □ **www.corian.com**

4 Simple white table with a tough white lacquer finish. For a classic white table, see the Maui table (1996) by Vico Magistretti □ **www.kartell.it**

5 Standard pine floorboards painted with a pale gray floor paint □ for paint, including floor paint, see the Directory of Suppliers on pages 152–55

Kong Barstool (2003) by Philippe Starck
□ **www.emeco.net**

Bombo (1997) by Stefano Giovannoni
□ **www.magisdesign.com**

Polo (1973) by Robin Day
□ **www.loftonline.net**

Grand by Börje Johanson
□ **www.johansondesign.se**

W.W. Stool (1994) by Philippe Starck
□ **www.vitra.com**

Cornflake by Mårten Claesson, Eero Koivisto
& Ola Rune □ **www.offecct.se**

Perch (1964) by Robert Propst
□ **www.hermanmiller.com**

Model No. 200, Sella (1957) by Achille &
Pier Giacomo Castiglioni □ **www.zanotta.it**

Order of the day

by KSR Architects

www.ksra.co.uk

Generations of piecemeal extensions, which had gradually crept farther and farther into the garden, were demolished to make way for this contemporary structure. Where once there was a jumble of add-ons now stands one beautifully finished space across the entire width of the house, providing the family with room for a kitchen, dining area, and soft seating, all looking over the large garden. The threshold is marked by three huge sliding glass panels, which span the $19^1/2$-foot opening, which leads on to a decked terrace.

1 Generous natural sunlight falls into the kitchen through this large, custom-designed ceiling rooflight □ **www.ksra.co.uk**

2 Nexus 111 wall-mounted spotlights in matte white □ **www.lightcorporation.com**

3 Ceiling-recessed speakers □ **www.bwspeakers.com**

4 Aluminum sliding doors, consisting of three panels, each $6^1/2$ feet wide □ **for architectural glass, see the Directory of Suppliers on pages 152–55**

5 Oversized 400 x 400mm ($15^3/4$") tiles in Bianco satin white make a refreshing change from their smaller cousins □ **for tiles, see the Directory of Suppliers on pages 152–55**

6 Black Zimbabwean granite worktop □ **for stone worktops, see the Directory of Suppliers on pages 152–55** □ Stone like this should be given a protective seal to prevent staining, so ask your supplier for advice. Many stone specialists suggest using Lithofin products, which include sealants and cleaners □ **www.lithofin.de**

7 Custom-made kitchen, including island with solid oak countertop □ **for kitchen furniture, see the Directory of Suppliers on pages 152–55**

8 Eucalyptus decking □ **for wooden decking, see the Directory of Suppliers on pages 152–55**

9 Aluminum trench heating □ **www.hcp-unilock.co.uk**

10 Solid oak floorboards □ **for wood flooring, see the Directory of Suppliers on pages 152–55**

Lyra bar stool with beech seat (1994), Design Group Italia □ **www.magisdesign.com**

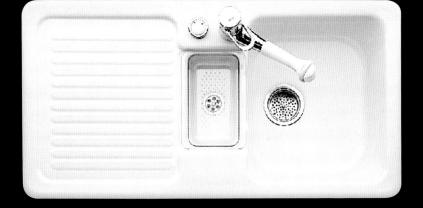

Condor 60 by Villeroy & Boch
▫ **www.villeroy-boch.com**

Cisterna by Villeroy & Boch
▫ **www.villeroy-boch.com**

Model No. DB116R by Smeg
▫ **www.smeg.it**

Anice by Antonia Astori
▫ **www.driade.com**

Luna by Villeroy & Boch
▫ **www.villeroy-boch.com**

Urban order
by Consarc Architects
with Bluestone Kitchens

www.consarc.co.uk □

www.bluestonekitchens.co.uk

A streamlined kitchen in an open-plan living space. This kitchen is designed in a galley style, with a single run of cabinets and appliances: it is compact and efficient for city living. The white cabinets looks particularly handsome with the stainless steel appliances and accessories. The entire kitchen is set deep in the apartment, close to the dining area, leaving the naturally lit part of the home for the main living space.

1 Under-cabinet lighting by Delta Light □ **www.deltalight.com**

2 Cox faucet □ **www.paini.com**

3 All the appliances, including the built-in oven, vent, and stainless steel refrigerator, are by Zanussi □ **www.zanussi.com**

Carisma circular stainless steel sink and drainer □ **www.carron.com**

Kuji White Range modular kitchen system □ **www.bluestonekitchens.co.uk**

Model No. BBX 651, Beach by David Goodwin
□ **www.franke.com**

Alien series, Model No. BX25.5SS by Baumatic
□ **www.baumatic.com**

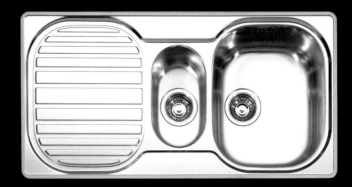

Model No. CPX 651, Compact (1979) by Franke
□ **www.franke.com**

Model No. MTG 651, Mythos by F.A. Porsche
□ **www.franke.com**

Triano by Villeroy & Boch
□ **www.villeroy-boch.com**

KV1 by Arne Jacobsen
□ www.vola.dk

Wall-fixed white kitchen units □
www.boffi.com

Kitchen drama

by Ann Boyd Design

e-mail: ann@annboyd-design.co.uk

The fashion-designer owner of this extremely grand 1870s home is a great host and loves to cook. The kitchen occupies what was originally a bedroom. Because the house is historically important, all original ornate detailing, with pretty moldings, had to remain intact and untouched. The client's brief was for generous work surfaces and a sociable space where he could talk to his guests while preparing the food. He wanted the room to combine modern kitchen fixtures with his collection of antiques, including the crystal chandelier and Elizabethan portrait, along with an old Irish oak table and chairs.

1 An antique iron and crystal chandelier makes an interesting contrast with the contemporary style of kitchen. Among makers of contemporary-style pendant lamps are Louis Poulsen □ www.louis-poulsen.com □ and Flos □ www.flos.net □ More traditional glass pendants made with world-famous Murano glass can be found at □ www.glasschandeliers.com

2 On the wall are cast metal mast lights from a traditional chandlers shop; they cast a powerful downlight. Among makers of such traditional ship's lighting is □ www.davey.co.uk

3 Vario toaster (1946) by Max Gort-Barten □ www.dualit.com

4 The island has a particularly beautiful stainless steel top with integral sink and comprises a sheer, inbuilt cooktop, and two dishwashers. The system has white acrylic doors □ www.boffi.com

5 The floor is finished in natural oak planks, 8 inches wide, which complement the room's generous proportions □ for wood flooring, see the Directory of Suppliers on pages 152–55

Triflow Doric by Franke
□ **www.franke.com**

Model No. MF2 by Smeg
□ **www.smeg.it**

Qube Sink Mixer by Bristan
□ **www.bristan.com**

Tara Classic by Sieger Design
□ **www.dornbracht.com**

Minta by Grohe
□ **www.grohe.com**

KV1 by Arne Jacobsen
□ **www.vola.dk**

HV1 by Arne Jacobsen
□ **www.vola.dk**

Tara wall-mounted by Sieger Design
□ **www.dornbracht.com**

Fusion Sink Mixer by Bristan
□ **www.bristan.com**

Zedra by Grohe
□ **www.grohe.com**

Brushed stainless steel handles from the Modric Range (1965),
Alan Tye □ **www.allgood.co.uk**

Bombo bar stools in green ABS plastic (1997),
Stefano Giovannoni □ **www.magisdesign.com**

Wassily chair in black leather (1925),
Marcel Breuer □ **www.knollint.com**

Informal dining
by Paul Mullins Associates

www.paulmullins.co.uk

The basement of this 1863 London townhouse
had been a collection of small rooms including
a home office at the front, living room at the
back, and kitchen in a brick extension. The designer's idea to improve the quality of the
space was to remove walls (achieved by strengthening the foundations and then inserting
steel beams over the openings), build in a sleek wood-finish kitchen, and make an ideal
informal entertaining space. The former kitchen extension is now a laundry space, keeping
noisy machines out of earshot. The palette of materials is simply white plastered walls and
wood. Splashes of color have been added by the lime green chairs and stools.

1 A brass-framed, gray slate gas fireplace, probably dating from
the 1960s, was moved here from the front room of the house. The
fireplace is elevated to become a focal point of the room. When not
in use, it is filled with a string of sparkling white Christmas tree lights
□ **for architectural salvage, including fireplaces, see the Directory of
Suppliers on pages 152–55**

2 Custom-made solid oak dining table, nearly 8 feet in length,
designed by
Paul Mullins □ **www.paulmullins.co.uk**

3 Series 7 Model No. 3107 chair (1955) by Arne Jacobsen. A range of
chairs constructed from molded plywood. The legs are made of mirror
chromed or satin chromed steel tubing. Series 7 is available in a wide
range of lacquer or lazur colors, as well as in natural veneers: maple,
beech, ash, cherry, and nut. The series includes chairs with arms, swivel
chairs on casters and a pedestal chair, plus a string of accessories
□ **www.fritzhansen.com**

4 A hardwearing, prefinished oak flooring system. It proved to be
ideal in an older property, as it is flexible enough to fit where floors
are not even or level □ **for wood flooring, see the Directory of
Suppliers on pages 152–55**

5 Large oven, oven-microwave, cooktop, and hood all from Neff
□ **www.neff.co.uk**

6 Custom-made oak kitchen with a plywood and stainless steel
countertop, designed by Paul Mullins □ **www.paulmullins.co.uk**

7 KV1 one-handle kitchen faucet (1969) by Arne Jacobsen.
□ **www.vola.com**

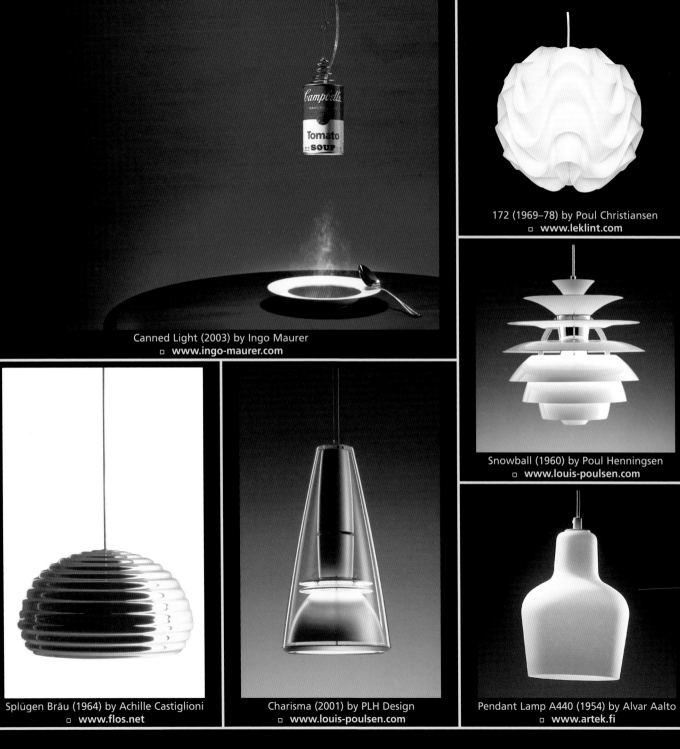

Canned Light (2003) by Ingo Maurer
□ **www.ingo-maurer.com**

172 (1969–78) by Poul Christiansen
□ **www.leklint.com**

Snowball (1960) by Poul Henningsen
□ **www.louis-poulsen.com**

Splügen Bräu (1964) by Achille Castiglioni
□ **www.flos.net**

Charisma (2001) by PLH Design
□ **www.louis-poulsen.com**

Pendant Lamp A440 (1954) by Alvar Aalto
□ **www.artek.fi**

Model No. HL3S81, Le Tre Streghe (1981) by
Guenther Leuchtmann □ **www.tecnolumen.de**

Cina, Rodolfo Dordoni (now discontinued); for similar, see □ **www.flos.net**

Light touch
by Ash Sakula Architects
www.ashsak.com

The key to this design was to respect the character of the room; it is large and high-ceilinged, with a bay window overlooking the rear garden. Before it was bought by its current owners, this nineteenth-century townhouse had been chopped up for multiple occupancy and divided crudely into separate dwellings. Their task was to restore the place back to a family home. In the large bay window sits the dining table, and flanking the window on the other side is a pair of refrigerators. Meanwhile the kitchen has been stowed away as simply as possible with a run of cabinets and accessories, plus an island. The wall-fixe cabinets are finished in an incredibly tough white material, while the island features aluminum drawers.

1 Custom-made kitchen cabinets are tailor-made to fit the space. The doors are finished with WISA-Van, a highly durable panel material set on plywood, more usually
to be found lining delivery trucks, which is a weather and impact resistant polyester glassfiber resin □ **www.wisa.upm-kymmene.com**

2 Custom-made stainless steel kitchen sink and work surface, which compose one continuous, and hygienic, run
□ **for kitchen furniture, see the Directory of Suppliers on pages 152–55**

3 The island has an iroko countertop and drawers fronted with reeded aluminum. Behind here are shelves for large and awkward kitchen items. Most exciting of all, the island also features underneath lighting, which gives the unit an ethereal quality and makes it appear to float in space □ **for lighting, see the Directory of Suppliers on pages 152–55**

4 Solid maple floorboards are used for a warm but light-colored and durable finish □ **for wood flooring, see the Directory of Suppliers on pages 152–55**

5 In addition to the two pendant lamps, the kitchen features small pools of task lighting—low-voltage lamps have been used around the sink area and are concealed behind the magnet message board. More small fixtures are used in an interesting way under the shelving. For contemporary light fixtures, see Erco □ **www.erco.com** □ and Wila □ **www.wila.com**

• Plastic and glass-fiber baths were once considered cheap and tacky, but the latest acrylic models are becoming popular among those who prefer to avoid cold metal bathtub sides; spa and whirlpool models are also gaining favor.

• Showering is no longer a simple wash. Everything from flexible hand-held showers to sophisticated multi-jet systems and combined water and steam treatment is available to enhance the experience.

• Countertop sinks are stylish; glass and steel sinks require regular cleaning to keep them looking their best.

• Good-quality, stylish faucets can transform economy fixtures.

• If children or elderly people use the bathroom, build in grab rails and nonslip surfaces.

• Some storage is useful for cleaning materials, toilet paper, and cosmetics; store medicines in a lockable cabinet.

A bathroom is no longer purely a functional space; there is a fresh emphasis on it as a place of relaxation and renewal. The bathroom's new elevated status can be measured by the amount of space we are prepared to devote to it. It is quite routine for main bedrooms to have a bathroom en suite; for adults and children to have of luxury. Among the most luxurious touches are large, powerful showers, steam rooms, fully-tiled wet-room spaces, whirlpool baths, floor-to-ceiling tiling—especially marble—and pairs of matching sinks. Added to this are high-quality controllable lighting and built-in music speakers. When planning a new bathroom, consider who will be

BATHROOMS

separate bathrooms; for spare bedrooms to be transformed into wetrooms; and for spaces to be carved out to make extra showers and powder rooms. Among the greatest influences on the new look is the hotel bathroom. Hotel designers are not just inspiring space engineers; they have also devised ways of adding an ever-greater sense using the space and how they like to wash—an early-morning shower user who prefers an invigorating start to the day or an evening bath taker who wants to relax and unwind. Children and old people may need to be provided for, too, by making sure there are secure grab rails to aid movement, no sharp corners, and nonslip surfaces.

Woodline 2 (2002) by Giampaolo Benedini
▫ **www.agapedesign.it**

Newson (2003) by Marc Newson
▫ **www.art-design-sculpture.co.uk**

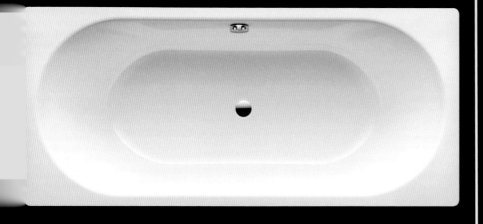

Classic by Kaldewei
▫ **www.kaldewei.com**

Spoon (1999) by Giampaolo Benedini
▫ **www.agapedesign.it**

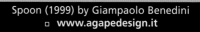

Bathroom with a view
by Denton Corker Marshall Architects
www.dcm-group.com

While most bathrooms have small windows or none at all, this has an entire wall of floor-to-ceiling glass and is a room with a view. With almost monastic simplicity the freestanding bathtub is complemented by the white ceramic sink sitting on its wooden shelf. The shade is an ingenious detail—pull it up for modesty's sake as you climb into the tub; then, once in, the bather can lower and open the window to enjoy the view over the local park.

1 Built-in walnut wood storage space designed by the architect □ **www.dcm-group.com**

2 Smart shade designed to be pulled upward. The screen can be in place while the bather climbs into the bath and then lowered for views over the park □ **for shades, see the Directory of Suppliers on pages 152–55**

3 Walnut wood shelf, which ties in with the cabinet, designed by the architect □ **www.dcm-group.com**

4 The surface of the solid concrete floor has been ground to a smooth and polished finish □ **for concrete flooring, see the Directory of Suppliers on pages 152–55**

132 wall-fixed faucet with long spout (1969), Arne Jacobsen □ **www.vola.com**

KV4 three-hole faucet with hand shower (1969), Arne Jacobsen □ **www.vola.com**

Architec Series circular white ceramic sink □ **www.duravit.com**

Esprit freestanding bathtub □ **www.bathstore.com**

Happy D. (1999) by Sieger Design
□ www.duravit.com

Mood (2000) by Mårten Claesson, Eero Koivisto & Ola Rune
□ www.boffi.com

Starck 3 Rectangular Bathtub (2002) by
Philippe Starck □ www.duravit.com

Aveo by Conran & Partners
□ www.villeroy-boch.com

Soikko by Durat
□ www.durat.com

Tara Classic wall-mounted faucet (1991),
Sieger Design □ **www.dornbracht.com**

I Fiumi Po solid limestone tub (1999),
Claudio Silvestrin □ **www.boffi.com**

Tara Classic faucet with showerhead (1991),
Sieger Design □ **www.dornbracht.com**

Pool of calm
by Claesson Koivisto Rune
www.claesson-koivisto-rune.se

Like bathing in a rockpool, this freestanding
oval bathtub has a magical quality. It takes center
stage in the bathroom of this refurbished grand
city-center apartment, where the architects
wanted to create as oasis of calm for bathing and
resting. Because of its tremendous weight,
however, the floor of this fourth-floor apartment
had to be strengthened with steel before the tub
could be craned into place through a window.
This room is the height of luxury; along with the
smooth, limestone bathtub and sandstone floor,
there is a built-in walnut-clad sauna room. The
use of natural materials and neutral colors
ensures that this is a tranquil place.

1 Tiny ceiling-recessed low-voltage halogen light
fittings are supplemented by this intriguing light, set into
the base of a wall niche. There's a monastic feel to this
feature which is entirely in tune with the minimalism of
the room □ **for lighting, see the Directory of Suppliers
on pages 152–55**

2 Custom-made tubular steel towel rail designed by the
architects, Mårten Claesson, Eero Koivisto, and Ola Rune.
A contemporary interpretation of the traditional wood
towel rail, it is related to Beckham, the larger. tubular
steel clothes hanging rail, also designed by the architects
□ **www.david.se**

3 Custom-made wall-fixed, walnut wood cabinet
designed by the architects. It provides storage space and
holds the sink □ **www.claesson-koivisto-rune.se**

4 Off-white ceramic mosaic tiles. The tiny squares
complement the geometry of the room's other finishes
and fixtures—rectangular storage units, square floor tiles,
and the oval bathtub □ **for tiles, see the Directory of
Suppliers on pages 152–55**

5 Swedish Gotland sandstone flooring in square tiles,
which have been sealed to prevent staining by water
□ **for stone flooring, see the Directory of Suppliers on
pages 152–55**

Il Bagno by Stefano Giovannoni
□ **www.ilbagno.alessi.com**

Viceversa by Benedini Associati
□ **www.agapedesign.it**

Vaioduo Oval by Kaldewei
□ **www.kaldewei.com**

Starck 1 Oval Bathtub by Philippe Starck
□ **www.duravit.com**

INXX faucet with chrome finish
□ **www.moraarmatur.se**

Tonga double-ended bathtub in a tiled
surround □ **www.sanycces.es**

Come on in
by Rahel Belatchew Lerdell
www.rbarchitecture.com

An inviting bathtub with picture window. This
room is on the first floor of a contemporary-style,
new frame house, which has been constructed on
a difficult sloping, rocky hillside. The conventional
floor plan of a house has been transposed, with
the main living area positioned upstairs to make
best use of natural sunlight and views. The first
floor is quiet and private. This bathroom is not
overlooked. It is simple but comfortable, featuring
an inviting double-ended bathtub, wall niches for
candles, and soft towels close at hand.

1 Called Floor, these extra-long rectangular white
ceramic tiles are extremely handsome and slightly
reminiscent of igloo-packed snow. However, despite
being all white, the room feels serene, rather than chilly.
In contrast with the wall tiles, the floor is finished in the
same style of tile, but they are brown-black in color
□ **www.ascot.it**

2 0829 aluminum doorknob □ **www.fsb.de**

Minuetto (2002) by Benedini Associati
□ **www.agapedesign.it**

Drop-in Basin by Stefano Giovannoni
□ **www.ilbagno.alessi.com**

Glass Bowl by Avante
□ **www.avantebathrooms.com**

Starck 1 Washbasin by Philippe Starck
□ **www.duravit.com**

Foster Washbasin with Pedestal (1999) by Norman Foster
□ **www.duravit.com**

Tara showerhead with dual controls and hand-held attachment (1991), Sieger Design □ **www.dornbracht.com**

Tara wall-mounted faucet (1991), Sieger Design □ **www.dornbracht.com**

Scola white ceramic sink □ **www.duravit.com**

Pooled resources
by Project Orange
www.projectorange.com

Instead of opting for a separate en-suite bath-room away from their children, the clients for this project wanted a large bathroom that could be shared by the whole family. The generous space has given them room for a pair of large sinks and a luxurious double shower, as seen in the mirror reflection, which is bathed in plenty of natural sunlight pouring through the acid-etched glass rooflight. Two clear glass circles in this rooflight provide views of the sky. For an added sense of luxury, and to reduce its impact on the room, the bathtub has been sunk into the floor, and the room is lined with stone.

1 Unusually, the floor and walls have been lined with Sera blue limestone. This gives the room a wonderful sheer finish and tranquil feel □ **for stone flooring, see the Directory of Suppliers on pages 152–55**

2 Recessed square wall lights called Side are used throughout this room, above the toilet and bidet, and built into the top of the wall around the skylight □ **www.kreon.com**

3 A neat doubled-ended white bathtub with central faucet, set into the floor. Lowering the level of the tub, is a clever design device, which makes it seem more luxurious and has the added benefit of reducing the tub's visual impact on the room □ **www.duravit.com**

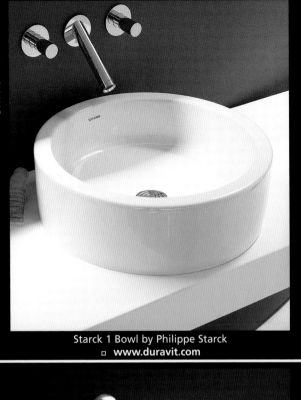

Starck 1 Bowl by Philippe Starck
□ **www.duravit.com**

Natural Stone Model 14 by Avante
□ **www.avantebathrooms.com**

Vero Washbasin by Duravit
□ **www.duravit.com**

Starck 2 Washbasin by Philippe Starck
□ **www.duravit.com**

Viceversa by Benedini Associati
□ **www.agapedesign.it**

Colorline Rectangular Basin by Villeroy & Boch
□ **www.villeroy-boch.com**

Wall-fixed, double-arm illuminated magnifying mirror in chrome □ www.samuel-heath.com

Aria white ceramic sink □ www.bathstore.com

As nature intended
by Phil Simmons at Simmons Interiors
www.simmonsinteriors.com

A minimalist interior incorporating dramatic lighting and textures was the brief for the refurbishment of this bathroom and entire riverside apartment. Materials used throughout the home are luxurious, from the curved glass wall and limestone floor at the entrance and custom-made cherry wood furniture and closets in the bedroom to the cherry wood and stainless steel kitchen. The bathroom is equally elegant, with its neat pair of countertop sinks, sitting on a stone bench, limestone-clad walls, and teak flooring.

1 Square, ceiling-recessed downlighters □ www.deltalight.com

2 Fittings on glass door to room and shower screen □ www.dorma.com

3 Space three-piece wall-mounted faucets with chrome spout □ www.bathstore.com

4 Myson MRR4 chrome towel-warming rail □ www.myson.co.uk

5 Limestone wall tiles. When using stone in bathrooms and kitchens, always check with the supplier for advice on appropriate finishes to prevent staining □ for tiles, see the Directory of Suppliers on pages 152–55

6 Flooring under the sinks in Elterwater Cumbrian stone, a green stone with lighter-colored veining □ for stone flooring, see the Directory of Suppliers on pages 152–55

7 Zero Light WC, wall-hung toilet with heavy-duty white seat □ www.bathstore.com

8 Floor-inset circular uplighters □ www.deltalight.com

9 Teak floor in a slatted design □ for wood flooring, see the Directory of Suppliers on pages 152–55

Starck 1 Washbasin by Philippe Starck
□ **www.duravit.com**

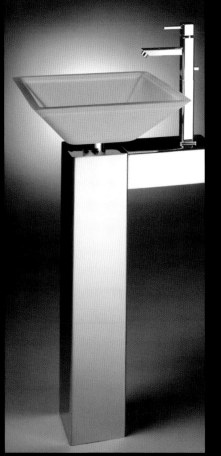

Square Bowl by Avante
□ **www.avantebathrooms.com**

Dreamscape Washbasin by Duravit
□ **www.duravit.com**

Colorline Square Basin by Villeroy & Boch
□ **www.villeroy-boch.com**

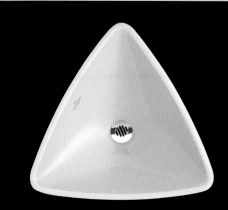

Colorline Triangular Basin by Villeroy & Boch
□ **www.villeroy-boch.com**

Natural Stone Model 13 by Avante
□ **www.avantebathrooms.com**

Metropole Basin by Christo Lefroy Brooks
□ **www.lefroybrooks.com**

Happy D. (1999) by Sieger Design
□ **www.duravit.com**

Wall-fixed extending mirror in chrome
□ www.samuel-heath.com

Axor Starck Widespread Set,
Philippe Starck □ www.hansgrohe.com

Stainless steel circular sink
□ www.agapedesign.it

A machine for bathing
by Groupe l'Arche with
Wessel von Loringhoven of CasaNova
email: archeplan@larche.ch

During the refurbishment of his home, the client commissioned the architect to create a tough, masculine style of bathroom with a splash of luxury. Rich stone and wood are used to line the space and make a deluxe cabin. Alongside these very obviously natural materials, complete with their grain and vein, a finely tuned industrial aesthetic is added with the exquisitely machined pair of stainless-steel sinks and faucets, the tall, vertical radiator, and the smaller accessories, including the extending mirror and towel rail.

1 Green granite with a delicate white vein is used to line walls and stand as the bathtub side panel. Granite is an extremely tough stone, available around the world □ **for tiles, see the Directory of Suppliers on pages 152–55**

2 Stainless steel vertical radiator, ideal for warming bath towels. For similar radiators, see Zehnder □ **www.zehnder.ws** □ and Imperial □ **www.imperialtowelrails.com**

3 Holes have been drilled into the granite, partly for decoration but also to encourage air circulation, essential in the damp atmosphere of a bathroom □ **for tiles, see the Directory of Suppliers on pages 152–55**

4 Teak—a traditional material for ships' decks because of its durability, especially when exposed to water—is used for flooring and appears again on the walls, this time used vertically to frame the built-in cabinets □ **for wood flooring, see the Directory of Suppliers on pages 152–55**

Axor Starck Mixer by Philippe Starck
□ **www.hansgrohe.com**

Axor Starck Puro Mixer by Philippe Starck
□ **www.hansgrohe.com**

Tara Basin Bridge Mixer by Sieger Design
□ **www.dornbracht.com**

Circa 29 Pillar Taps by Sottini
□ **www.sottini.co.uk**

Tara Basin Mixer by Sieger Design
□ **www.dornbracht.com**

Jo Mono Basin by Christo Lefroy Brooks
□ **www.lefroybrooks.com**

Jo Mono Wall-mounted by Christo Lefroy
Brooks □ **www.lefroybrooks.com**

Atrio High Bowl Mixer by Grohe
□ **www.grohe.com**

Murano Waterfall by Hansa
□ **www.hansa.de**

Alchemy Dual Control Basin Mixer by
Sottini □ **www.sottini.co.uk**

Light fantastic
by Jean Nouvel
www.jeannouvel.fr

Many of the best ideas for bathrooms at home are drawn from bathrooms in hotels. This is an inspiring guest bathroom in a Swiss hotel, called The Hotel, designed by Jean Nouvel. The design is conceived to "celebrate simplicity and spirituality as much as it does elegance and refinement. The central idea is to create something quite unlike anything before that provides guests with a magical, exciting and unforgettable feeling." The bathroom is dark and womblike, with light concentrated around the sink and mirror area. The lights set into the mirror are reminiscent of theatrical dressing rooms.

1 Indirect light to the ceiling by compact fluorescent tube hidden behind a mirror-finish aluminum panel. This type of lamp is widely available and produced by all big-name lamp manufacturers □ **for lighting, see the Directory of Suppliers on pages 152–55**

2 A custom-made design, which sets a quartet of oversize lightbulbs at the corners of this mirror □ **for lighting, see the Directory of Suppliers on pages 152–55**

3 A range of stainless steel accessories, including the door handle □ **www.dline.com**

4 Custom-made countertop by Jean Nouvel, with integral basins in Corian □ **www.corian.com**

5 The flooring combines reconstituted stone tiles called Silestone white □ **www.silestone.com** and jatoba wood, also known as Brazilian cherry □ **for wood flooring, see the Directory of Suppliers on pages 152–55**

KV10 three-hole faucets, Arne Jacobsen □ **www.vola.dk**

Bath and Shower Tap by Stefano Giovannoni
□ **www.ilbagno.alessi.com**

Axor Citterio Trim Tub Set by
Antonio Citterio □ **www.hansgrohe.com**

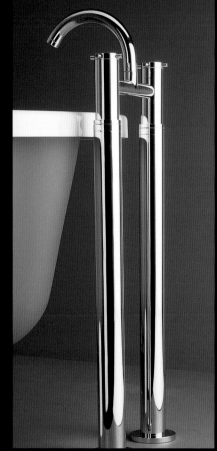

Floor-standing Bath Tap by Stefano Giovannoni
□ **www.ilbagno.alessi.com**

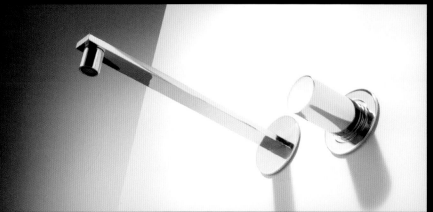

Elle Wall-mounted Bath Tap by Bonomi
□ **www.bonomi.it**

Alchemy Standpipes Bath Filler by Sottini
□ **www.art-design-sculpture.co.uk**

Elle Bath Tap by Bonomi
□ **www.bonomi.it**

Axor Starck Widespread Set by Philippe Starck
□ **www.hansgrohe.com**

Tara Classic faucet (1991),
Sieger Design □ **www.dornbracht.com**

Tara Classic faucet (1991),
Sieger Design □ **www.dornbracht.com**

Centroform Oval double-ended steel bathtub with
central drain opening □ **www.kaldewei.com**

Starck 1 series white ceramic sink,
Philippe Starck □ **www.duravit.com**

Fluid space

by Form Design Architecture

www.form-architecture.co.uk

When the owner took over this penthouse, it was an awkward-shaped shell. From the difficult spaces, the architect created an intriguing apartment of flowing spaces, each with a distinct character. The bathroom is sited on the mezzanine level, next to the main bedroom, a haven away from the formal, public spaces below. The idea was to create an interesting space with beautiful, luxurious finishes. The double shower with fiber optics is inspired—bathing the user with light as well as water.

1 Custom-made shower designed by the architect. The shower head incorporates fiber optics to bathe the user in light as well as water □ **www.form-architecture.co.uk** □ This double shower runs along the wall opposite the tub and sinks and has a glass screen □ **for architectural glass, see the Directory of Suppliers on pages 152–55**

2 Ceiling-recessed low-voltage halogen lamps. The crisp quality of light from these lamps is excellent in bathrooms where it adds sparkle to the reflective surfaces □ **for lighting, see the Directory of Suppliers on pages 152–55**

3 Whatever the mood, this bathroom is wired for sound, with speakers from the home's fully integrated sound system, which are concealed within the ceiling □ **www.bwspeakers.com**

4 Wall-mounted shower control □ **for bathroom fittings, see the Directory of Suppliers on pages 152–55**

5 A single length of Bateige Blue limestone ingeniously serves as the surround for the tub as well as the countertop for the pair of matching white ceramic sinks. Two recesses are lined with metal laminate for towel storage. The stone was sealed to make it waterproof □ **for stone tiles, see the Directory of Suppliers on pages 152–55**

6 Limestone floor tiles, treated with a water sealant recommended by the manufacturer □ **www.lithofin.de**

7 The sliding mirrored doors double as shutters to the window over the tub, and doors to the medicine cabinets on either side when open.

Amera Shower System by Grohe
□ **www.grohe.com**

Rainshower by Grohe
□ **www.grohe.com**

Axor Citterio Showerhead by Antonio Citterio
□ **www.hansgrohe.com**

Alchemy Overhead Shower by Sottini
□ **www.art-design-sculpture.co.uk**

Brunswick Showerhead by Christo Lefroy
Brooks □ **www.lefroybrooks.com**

Jo Headset Shower by Christo Lefroy
Brooks □ **www.lefroybrooks.com**

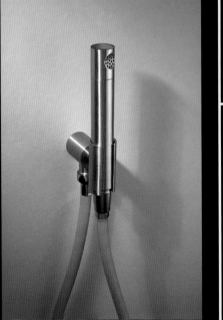

Jo Wall-mounted Shower by Christo
Lefroy Brooks □ **www.lefroybrooks.com**

Jo Exposed Shower Rose by Christo
Lefroy Brooks □ **www.lefroybrooks.com**

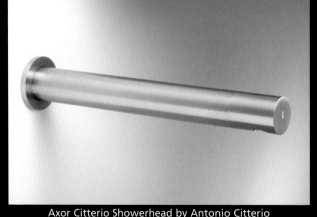

Axor Citterio Showerhead by Antonio Citterio
□ **www.hansgrohe.com**

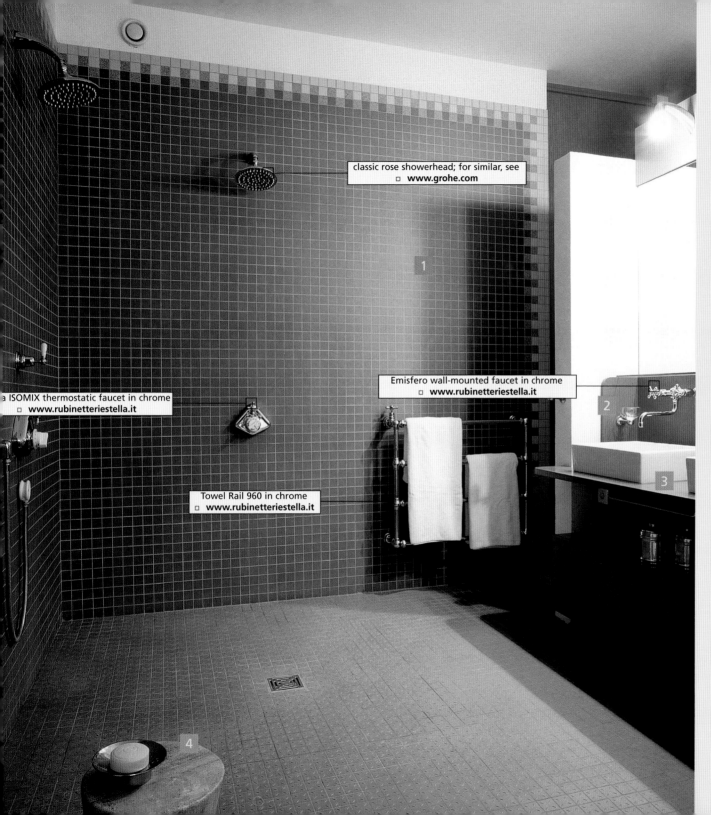

classic rose showerhead; for similar, see
□ **www.grohe.com**

a ISOMIX thermostatic faucet in chrome
□ **www.rubinetteriestella.it**

Emisfero wall-mounted faucet in chrome
□ **www.rubinetteriestella.it**

Towel Rail 960 in chrome
□ **www.rubinetteriestella.it**

A bigger splash
by Philippe Starck
www.philippe-starck.com

For anyone who loves showers, this is the perfect place for washing and pampering—a floor-to-ceiling, fully tiled wetroom. The huge showerheads guarantee a powerful and invigorating shower experience. Free from the constraints of poky shower stalls, and with twin showers and twin basins, there's even enough room to share the space with a friend. Unusually for a bathroom, the color scheme includes splashes of red.

1 Large-scale 2- x 2-inch black mosaic tiles have been used to line this wetroom from floor to ceiling
□ **www.winckelmans.com**

2 Roma tumbler holder in chrome with transparent glass tumbler □ **www.rubinetteriestella.it**

3 White ceramic square sink □ **www.duravit.com**

4 Stool made in stone □ **www.habitat.net**

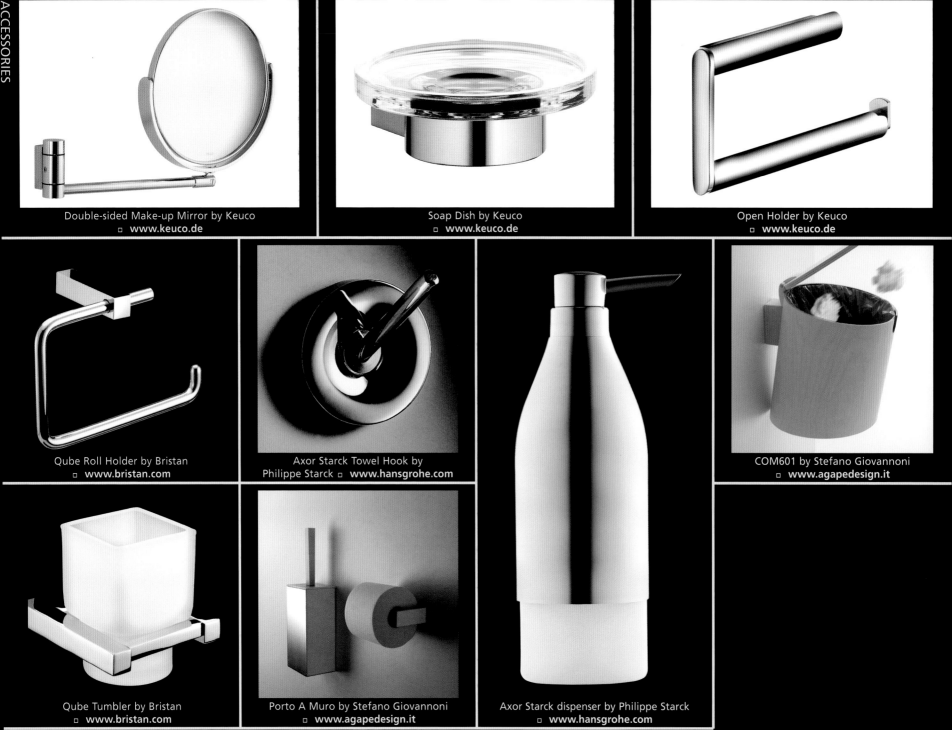

Double-sided Make-up Mirror by Keuco
▫ **www.keuco.de**

Soap Dish by Keuco
▫ **www.keuco.de**

Open Holder by Keuco
▫ **www.keuco.de**

Qube Roll Holder by Bristan
▫ **www.bristan.com**

Axor Starck Towel Hook by
Philippe Starck ▫ **www.hansgrohe.com**

COM601 by Stefano Giovannoni
▫ **www.agapedesign.it**

Qube Tumbler by Bristan
▫ **www.bristan.com**

Porto A Muro by Stefano Giovannoni
▫ **www.agapedesign.it**

Axor Starck dispenser by Philippe Starck
▫ **www.hansgrohe.com**

1

2

Medicine Cabinet in red lacquer (1992),
Thomas Ericksson □ **www.cappellini.it**

3

Single-lever chrome basin faucet
□ **www.hansgrohe.com**

4

5

Class cabin
by Simon Allford of
Allford Hall Monaghan Morris
www.ahmm.co.uk

A cabin-style, walnut-lined bathroom continues
the design theme in this remodeled apartment,
which is as classy as the A-deck cabins of a luxury
liner. The bathroom is compact but luxuriously
finished. The use of dark, richly patterned walnut
wood to line the walls is an unusual and
refreshing choice when light-colored bathrooms
are the norm. Cork flooring tiles, which are
readily available from all good flooring stores,
are sealed with a water- and stainproof acrylic
finish. Cork flooring enjoyed a heyday in the
1970s, but is used less often now; however, it is a
natural and sustainable material that is warm to
the touch and extremely hardwearing.

1 Walnut cladding □ **for wood, including cladding,
see the Directory of Suppliers on pages 152–55**

2 Wall-fixed extending and pivoting mirror in chrome
□ **www.samuel-heath.com**

3 An original Brionvega ts522 portable radio by
Marco Zanussi and Richard Sapper. A classic 1960s design
□ **www.brionvega.it**

4 Smart, rectangular-shaped, wall-mounted, white
ceramic basin which suits the masculine, clubby look
of this bathroom. Classic ranges can be found in the
products by Laufen □ **www.laufen.com**

5 Cabinet doorknob Modric 2501 in brushed
stainless steel □ **www.allgood.co.uk**

Alvita by Aestus
□ www.aestus-radiators.com

Hot Spring by Bisque
□ www.bisque.co.uk

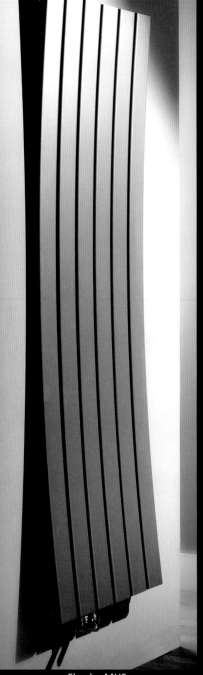

Flex by MHS
□ www.mhsboilers.com/radiators

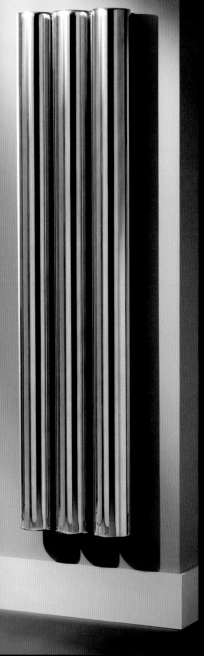

Big One by MHS
□ www.mhsboilers.com/radiators

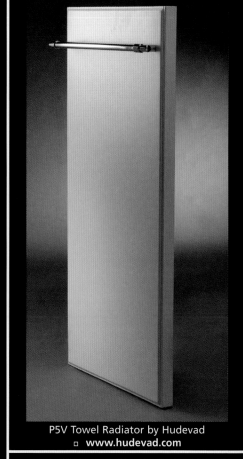

P5V Towel Radiator by Hudevad
□ www.hudevad.com

Hot Hoop by Bisque
□ www.bisque.co.uk

Cobra-Therm wall-mounted towel-warming radiator in chrome □ **www.bisque.co.uk**

BK10 one-handled faucet with hand shower (1959), Arne Jacobsen □ **www.vola.com**

Megaform Oval double-ended steel tub with central drain opening □ **www.kaldewei.com**

Remodeled townhouse
by Alison Brooks Architects
www.alisonbrooksarchitects.com

During the refurbishment of this 1970s townhouse, the bathroom was opened up to adjoin the bedroom. The architect conceived the bathroom as a piece of sculpture; it sits raised up on a limestone platform, and the curvy bathtub can be seen from the bed. Natural light falls onto the tub from a circular roof light. Throughout the house the fitted furniture has been designed by the architect and built in cherry wood.

1 A single sheet of toughened, sandblasted 12mm (½") glass makes an ideal shower enclosure. It looks particularly elegant because it has been set into metal channels sunk into the wall, ceiling, and floor, dispensing with the need to use a frame □ **for architectural glass, see the Directory of Suppliers on pages 152–55**

2 112 wall-mounted, one-handled faucet □ **www.vola.com**

3 BluToo plywood countertop circular sink with satin lacquer finish □ **www.minetti.de**

4 The shimmering bathtub surround is made in aluminum Formica, which has been laminated to a plywood backing. It is warmer to the touch than metal sheeting and doesn't attract fingermarks □ **www.formica.com**

5 Limestone flooring is best laid on a solid base, such as concrete. If it is laid on a wooden floor, the weight can be too great for joists, and the slight movement inevitable with wooden floors can disturb the grout and allow water to seep through the floor □ **for stone flooring, see the Directory of Suppliers on pages 152–55**

Hot Box by MHS
□ **www.mhsradiators.com**

O.J.C. (1991) by Giampaolo Benedini
□ **www.agapedesign.it**

Hylly by Durat
□ **www.durat.com**

Mirror cabinet by Keuco
□ **www.keuco.de**

Model No. M53280 by Stefano Giovannoni
□ **www.ilbagno.alessi.com**

Custom-made pendant lamp designed by the architect □ **www.foxlinton.com**

Tara wall-mounted faucet (1991), Sieger Design □ **www.dornbracht.com**

BetteStarlet double-ended white enameled tub □ **www.bette.de**

Art Deco style
by Fox Linton Associates
www.foxlinton.com

This extremely handsome bathroom was inspired by the great Art Deco period of the 1930s and uses a palette of luxurious materials, which have been chosen for rich pattern and strong contrasting light and dark shades—a characteristic of the period design. The materials include pale limestone and dark marble, while the addition of glass, walnut wood for the cabinets and a glint of stainless steel on light fixtures and taps adds to the richness. The design makes excellent use of space, finding room for twin sinks as well as shelving for towels. Take care when purchasing bathroom lighting for different countries around the world have their own regulations. Check that any lamps match the specification before you buy.

1 Marron honed chocolate marble used on the walls and floor □ **for stone flooring, see the Directory of Suppliers on pages 152–55**

2 Wallcovering by bathtub is a panel of white glass, which gives a luxurious and sheer finish □ **for architectural glass, see the Directory of Suppliers on pages 152–55**

3 Tara wall-mounted faucet (1991) by Sieger Design. A range that includes not only faucets, but also a selection of matching bathroom accessories, including storage units, soap holders, and mirrors □ **www.dornbracht.com**

4 Custom-made limestone countertop circular sink □ **for bathroom furniture, see the Directory of Suppliers on pages 152–55**

5 Custom-made countertop in otto beige limestone to contrast with marble used on the walls and floor □ **for stone worktops, see the Directory of Suppliers on pages 152–55**

6 Custom-made walnut under-sink storage cabinets designed by the architect □ **www.foxlinton.com**

• Whether it's a Victorian iron bedstead or a minimalist plinth, the style of bed will set the character for the room.

• We own more clothes and shoes than any previous generation. If you need more closet space, be sure to overestimate your needs by about 20 percent—or be ruthless in weeding out clothes you're tired of.

• Take care in selecting a mattress, and buy the best you can afford. As a rule, the more coils a mattress contains, the better it supports your body.

• A closet light is simple to achieve and so useful when searching for the right shirt or jacket.

• If daylight interrupts your sleep, fit a blackout shade to the inside of the window.

• Build in good lighting, around mirrors for dressing and for reading in bed.

reassuring coziness of a more traditionally furnished space, the bedroom should be restful and comfortable. The bed is a major element, which needs to be chosen with care. A good-quality mattress and box spring may not enhance the decor, sensuous, natural materials such as wood flooring, deep-pile rugs, gorgeous linens, soft blankets, and velvet throws. Although a bedroom is associated with mainly sleep, for most of us it is a multifunctional space used for dressing and making up, watching

BEDROOMS

but they will enhance one-third of your life and will last for years. The style of this piece of furniture will influence the look of the entire room; however, it is fun to play with contrasts—a huge, dark wood, Gothic-style bed could look magnificent in an otherwise minimally furnished room. As with bathrooms, interesting ideas television, meditating, working out, and even sometimes accommodating a home office. Lighting is especially important; ambient lighting is required for early mornings and evenings and can be achieved with pendant and/or wall lamps. However, additional lighting is needed by mirrors and is essential for reading in bed.

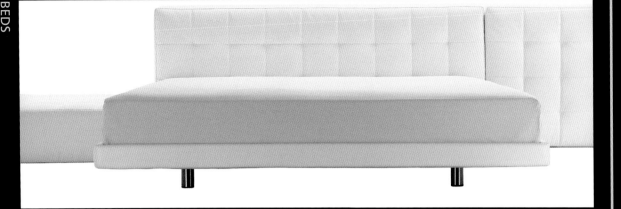

Model No. 1870, Alfa (2002) by Emaf Progetti
□ **www.zanotta.it**

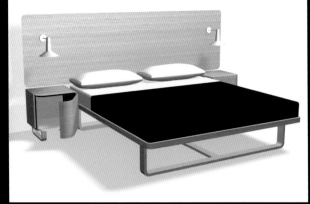

Drift by Michael Sodeau
□ **www.twentytwentyone.com**

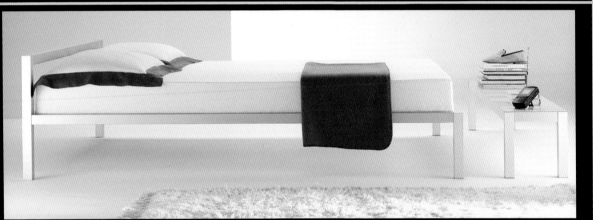

Aluminum Bed by Bruno Fattorini
□ **www.mdfitalia.it**

REM by Terence Woodgate
□ **www.scp.co.uk**

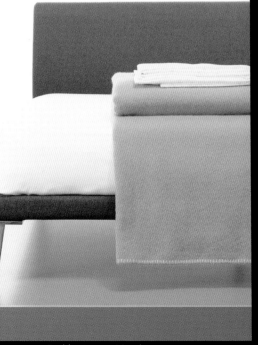

Bed by Jasper Morrison
□ **www.cappellini.it**

Rosy Angelis tripod floorlamp with cotton shade (1994),
Philippe Starck □ **www.flos.net**

Archimoon Soft table lamp in aluminum,
Philippe Starck □ **www.flos.net**

Leha bed with fabric-covered base on
aluminum feet □ **www.tisettanta.com**

Soft and soothing
by Harry Elson Architect

www.harryelson.com

Pale, neutral colors, soft upholstery materials, and wall-to-wall carpet, with details in natural wood have combined to make this an extremely inviting and restful bedroom. The house is built in a neo-Colonial style, and in deliberate contrast with the historic look of the exterior, the recent refurbishment has provided the young owners with sophisticated, contemporary interiors. The design idea was to simplify the interiors so that the personality of each space was created through the furniture and furnishings. This main bedroom is modern classic in style.

1 Pure cotton bed linens □ **www.frette.com**

2 Lugano, a useful end-of-bed bench, part of the Halifax range
□ **www.tisettanta.com**

3 Susanna, soft upholstered armchairs, by Vico Magistretti. They add a sense of luxury and calm to the room □ **www.depadova.it**

4 White shirred mink throw □ **www.frette.com**

5 Giro table (1997–99), by Anna Deplano. A circular, two-tier, caster-mounted steel-frame table □ **www.zanotta.it**

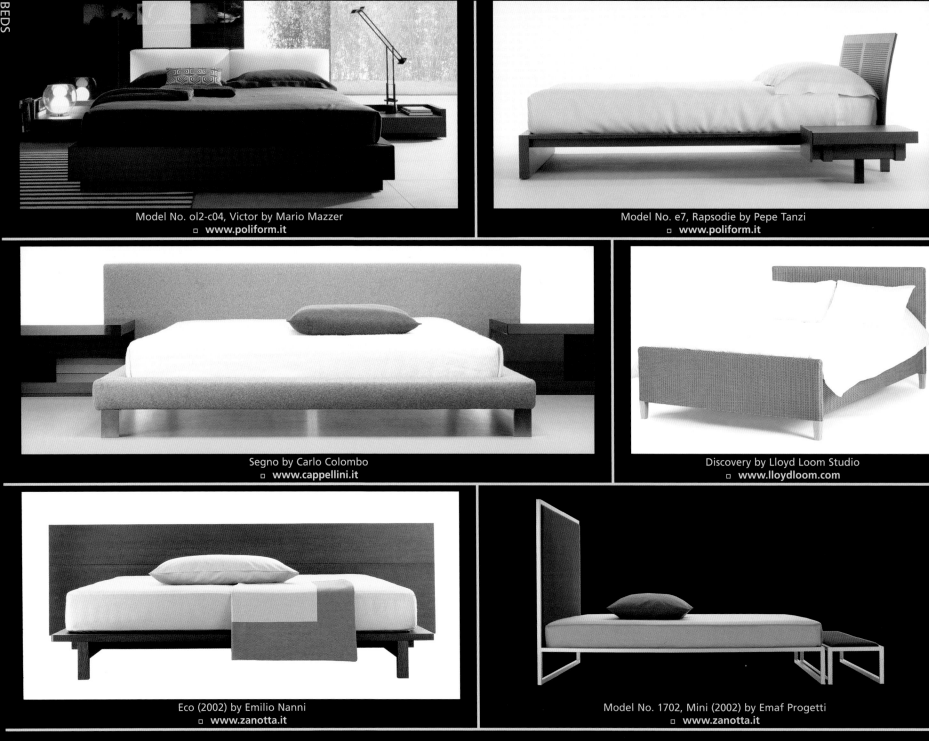

Model No. ol2-c04, Victor by Mario Mazzer
□ **www.poliform.it**

Model No. e7, Rapsodie by Pepe Tanzi
□ **www.poliform.it**

Segno by Carlo Colombo
□ **www.cappellini.it**

Discovery by Lloyd Loom Studio
□ **www.lloydloom.com**

Eco (2002) by Emilio Nanni
□ **www.zanotta.it**

Model No. 1702, Mini (2002) by Emaf Progetti
□ **www.zanotta.it**

Low-Pad easy chair (1999) in padded white leather and chrome, Jasper Morrison □ www.cappellini.it

Wenge wood-frame bed with headboard upholstered in gray moleskin felt □ www.poliform.it

Laid-back luxury

by Tara Bernerd of Target Living

www.targetliving.com

The brief for this bedroom was to create a "simple and fresh-looking" scheme to reflect the contemporary style of this home. It is an elegant courtyard house by leading British architect Sir Terry Farrell, in which the emphasis is on transparency, with huge sheets of floor-to-ceiling glass giving views into the pretty garden as well as through the whole house. The bedroom is furnished in a rich palette of materials, including leather and wenge wood, with plenty of horizontal lines—the long ottoman at the end of the bed and low-level easy chair—lending a tranquil air to the space.

1 Shashiko woven khaki cotton weave bedcover
□ www.donghia.com

2 Handmade cushion with shocking pink sequin border to add a splash of color □ **for home accessories, see the Directory of Suppliers on pages 152–55**

3 Custom-made brown crocodile-print leather ottoman designed by Tara Bernerd □ **www.targetliving.com**

4 Foldaway bedside tables, 1920s Lucite Perspex. For specialists in transparent furniture, see Bobo □ **www.bobodesign.co.uk**

5 Enormous white Perspex lamps. For a selection of beautiful white lamps, see the Shadows collection (1999) by Marcel Wanders □ **www.cappellini.it**

6 Shashiko woven khaki cotton, same material as bedcover
□ **www.donghia.com**

Oxygène Wardrobe System by Gautier
□ **www.gautier.fr**

Model No. po2-06, Senzafine New Entry Wardrobe by CR Poliform
□ **www.poliform.it**

BL451 (1997) by Marco Ferreri
□ **www.agapedesign.it**

Classic Linen Basket by Lloyd Loom Studio
□ **www.lloydloom.com**

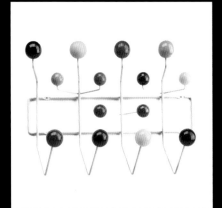

Hang-It-All (1953) by Charles & Ray Eames
□ **www.vitra.com**

Beckham (2000) by Mårten Claesson,
Eero Koivisto & Ola Rune □ **www.david.se**

Custom-made built-in storage, with tall, slim doors designed to give vertical emphasis to the space ☐ **www.renedekker.com**

Lumen floor lamp (1954) with white-painted metal frame ☐ **www.fontanaarte.it**

Compact living

by Rene Dekker

www.renedekker.com

This small studio apartment has been designed with big ambitions. The 270 square feet of space don't just function as a well-designed living space; they also have to work hard as an office and include reference to the client's Chinese heritage. Walls are lined from floor to ceiling with storage; on one wall, cabinets conceal a foldaway bed. Opposite, doors open to reveal a desk with drawers, a fax machine and modem, TV, and a sound system. In the center of the room there's a soft seating area and, with the bed folded up, space for a dining table and chairs. While the color scheme is pale taupe, the designer wanted to include a range of interesting textures, including polished plaster walls, soft carpet, voile Roman shades. Zesty color is added with rust-colored silk cushions and paintings.

1 Steel doorknobs ☐ **for architectural hardware, see the Directory of Suppliers on pages 152–55**

2 Natural Rope carpet, in a color called String ☐ **www.timpagecarpets.co.uk**

3 When the bed is pulled down from the wall, it reveals this pretty printed fabric panel, Les Cavaliers, designed by Manuel Canovas, from Colefax and Fowler ☐ **www.colefaxantiques.com**

4 Mechanism for raising and lowering the foldaway bed, by the architectural hardware expert Häfele ☐ **www.haefele.de**

5 A light cotton voile fabric from Nya Nordiska ☐ **www.nya.com**

6 Rust-colored silk made into Oriental-style cushions by Fox Linton Associates ☐ **www.foxlinton.com**

7 Bed linens by The Linen Mill, which has a sister company called The Leather Bed Company ☐ **www.thelinenmill.com**

8 Twenty ceiling-recessed, low-voltage halogen lamps were added to enable the owner to change the mood of the space with the use of dimmer switches ☐ **for lighting, see the Directory of Suppliers on pages 152–55**

Little Big Lamp (2003) by Ingo Maurer
▫ **www.ingo-maurer.com**

Berlin by Mårten Claesson, Eero Koivisto
& Ola Rune ▫ **www.atelje-lyktan.se**

Roatinno (1935) by Eileen Gray
▫ **www.classicon.com**

Floorlamp A809 (1959) by Alvar Aalto
▫ **www.artek.fi**

Stylos (1984) by Achille Castiglioni
▫ **www.flos.net**

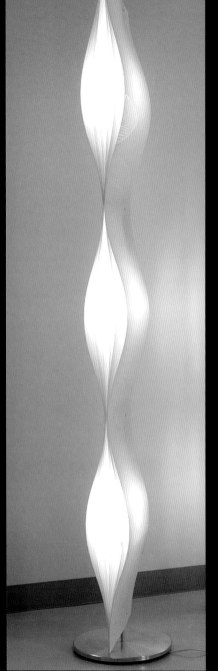

S-light by Hiroki Takada
▫ **www.tadakadesign.com**

Tolomeo aluminum wall lamp (1987), Michele de Lucchi & Giancarlo Fassina ▫ **www.artemide.com**

D line range, B102.0 pull handles (1970s), Knud Holscher ▫ **www.dline.com**

Maly beech wood and upholstered bed with aluminum feet and TV table (1983), Peter Maly ▫ **www.ligne-roset.com**

Reinvented space
by DSP Architects

www.dsparchitecture.co.uk

When the owner of this riverside apartment had the opportunity to buy and build on the roof space above, he decided to make the lower part of his duplex into a luxurious bedroom suite, complete with dressing room plus a guest room. Upstairs, a glass box addition was constructed for the new kitchen and dining and living area. The architect installed two beautiful bathrooms, complete with spa baths, and simple, finely detailed bedrooms. This main bedroom has glass sliding doors to the new dressing room and French doors to the terrace.

1 Tubular steel radiator; for similar see ▫ **www.hudevad.dk**

2 Solid white American oak, tongue-and-groove boards, 5 inches wide and with decorative V-joint. Eidely available flooring type ▫ **for wood flooring, see the Directory of Suppliers on pages 152-55**

3 Toughened, acid-etched glass on Hâfele Junior 80 sliding track ▫ **www.haefele.de**

4 The dressing room built-in-cabinets were custom designed and built using MDF doors which have been painted with eggshell oil paint applied by roller for a sheer finish ▫ **www.dsparchitecture.co.uk**

5 Unusual shades in woven aluminum ▫ **for blinds and shades, see the Directory of Suppliers on pages 152–55**

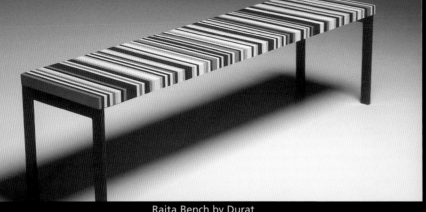

Raita Bench by Durat
□ **www.durat.com**

Fan Chair by Hiroki Takada
□ **www.tadakadesign.com**

Model No. CH28 (1951) by Hans J. Wegner
□ **www.carlhansen.com**

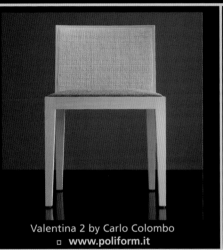

Valentina 2 by Carlo Colombo
□ **www.poliform.it**

Spring Back Chair by Matthew Bear &
Scott Moulton □ **www.unionstudio.com**

Knotted Chair (1996) by Marcel Wanders
□ **www.cappellini.it**

Urban Bench by Matthew Hilton
□ **www.scp.co.uk**

Model No. 280, Zig-zag Chair (1932–34) by
Gerrit Thomas Rietveld □ **www.cassina.it**

Charles bed (1998), an extension of the sofa range, Antonio Citterio □ www.bebitalia.it

Panton chair in red injection-molded plastic (1960), Verner Panton □ **www.vitra.com**

Prince AHA stool in white polypropylene, Philippe Starck □ **www.kartell.it**

Period piece
by Simon Siegel

www.atomicinteriors.co.uk

For many years Simon and Monica Siegel had known about and admired this stylish Modernist house built in central England, but when it eventually came on the market, the price tag was too high. However, when the potential buyer's bid fell through, they felt it was fate and made an offer, which was accepted. The house was designed in the 1960s by architect David Shelley, and has survived the years pretty much intact and unscathed by fad and fashion. It is furnished with the impressive postwar furniture collection owned by Simon Siegel, who is in the interior design and retail business and who lectures in design, and Monica Siegel, who is a translator. The bedroom overlooks a pretty stone courtyard garden in one direction and a luxurious indoor swimming pool in another.

1 The wall is lined in the original rosewood veneer
□ **for wood, including cladding, see the Directory of Suppliers on pages 152–55**

2 Vertical blind in a vibrant blue, inherited from the previous owner □ **for blinds and shades, see the Directory of Suppliers on pages 152–55**

3 Atollo table lamp (1977) by Vico Magistretti. Gives direct and diffuse light through an opaline blown Murano glass diffuser □ **www.oluce.com**

4 Bedside cabinet with drawers, built in and contemporary with the house □ **for furniture designers and makers, see the Directory of Suppliers on pages 152–55**

5 Eclisse table lamp (1966) by Vico Magistretti. Eclisse translates as "eclipse," and the light coming from the lamp is controlled by pulling a diffuser across the bulb opening □ **www.artemide.com**

6 Wool carpet, also in a vibrant blue, inherited from the previous owner □ **for carpets, see the Directory of Suppliers on pages 152–55**

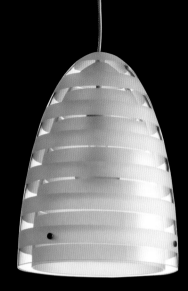

Luester (2003) by Ingo Maurer
□ **www.ingo-maurer.com**

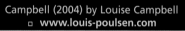

Campbell (2004) by Louise Campbell
□ **www.louis-poulsen.com**

Le Klint 173 (1969–78) by Poul Christiansen
□ **www.leklint.com**

Random Light (2002) by Monkey Boys
□ **www.moooi.com**

85 Lamps (1993) by Rodi Graumans
□ **www.droogdesign.nl**

Light Shade Shade (1999) by Jurgen Bey
□ **www.moooi.com**

Wo bist du, Edison, …? (1997) by
Ingo Maurer □ **www.ingo-maurer.com**

Le Klint 178 (1969–78) by Poul Christiansen
□ **www.leklint.com**

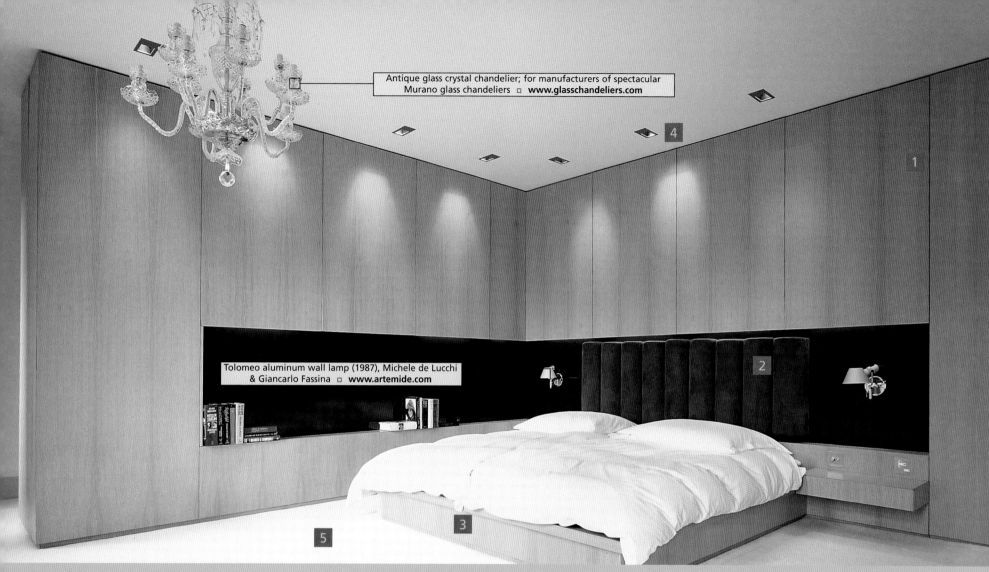

Antique glass crystal chandelier; for manufacturers of spectacular
Murano glass chandeliers □ **www.glasschandeliers.com**

Tolomeo aluminum wall lamp (1987), Michele de Lucchi
& Giancarlo Fassina □ **www.artemide.com**

Jet set chic
by Project Orange

www.projectorange.com

A retro-style bedroom has been created in the unlikely setting
of a Victorian house. The wraparound wall, in panels of white-
lacquered oak veneer, is a huge piece of furniture, which
incorporates a closet and storage cabinets accessed from the
back. Behind here is also an en-suite bathroom. The dark
horizontal band at bed level provides shelving space for books
on one wall and then turns at 90 degrees to become the
upholstered headboard. A glittering antique crystal chandelier,
a family heirloom, provides the final glamorous flourish.

1 The wraparound wall is custom designed by the architect using oak
veneer panels, which have been finished with a translucent white
lacquer. On the outer face of the wall are closets and storage space □
www.projectorange.com

2 The restful line created by the low horizontal band that frames the
bed is finished in a glossy dark charcoal-colored lacquer where it forms
a recess for books. Behind the bed, the padded headboard is
upholstered in a suedelike fabric called Glove □ **www.kvadrat.dk**

3 Bed, custom design by the architect □ **www.projectorange.com**

4 Recessed ceiling lights called Twin Slide, with two lamps
in each fixture for wall washing by Modular Lighting
□ **www.supermodular.com**

5 The floor covering is a neutral, stone-color wool carpet
□ **for carpets, see the Directory of Suppliers on pages 152–55**

Brera W (1992) by Achille Castiglioni
□ **www.flos.net**

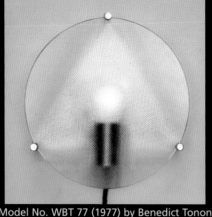

Model No. WBT 77 (1977) by Benedict Tonon
□ **www.tecnolumen.de**

Io (2004) by Merete Christensen & Bo Seedorff
□ **www.louis-poulsen.com**

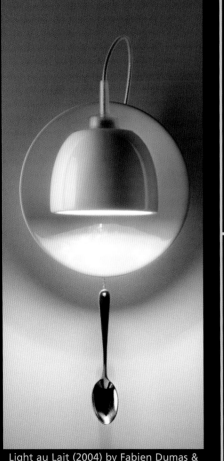

Lucellino (1992) by Ingo Maurer
□ **www.ingo-maurer.com**

Light au Lait (2004) by Fabien Dumas &
Ingo Maurer □ **www.ingo-maurer.com**

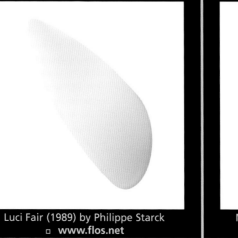

Luci Fair (1989) by Philippe Starck
□ **www.flos.net**

Noce T (1972) by Achille Castiglioni
□ **www.flos.net**

Romeo Babe wall lamp in aluminum (1998),
Philippe Starck □ **www.flos.net**

Slatted bed with wenge-colored veneer
□ **www.boconcept.com**

Basement oasis
by John Kerr Associates

www.johnkerrassociates.com

This luxurious basement bedroom and bathroom have been
created in what was, a century ago, a Jewish soup kitchen
serving 6,000 people every night. The intriguing and
handsome building, with its red brick and terracotta façade,
has now been transformed into apartments. The bedroom and
bathroom form part of a very spacious live/work duplex—the
upstairs, where the business of the day is conducted, is bright,
brisk, and open, while below it is a darker, restful retreat,
furnished with handsome dark furniture and rich materials.

1 Spiral Ribbon Chandelier made by stretching cotton over a
spiral frame □ **www.purves.co.uk**

2 Three-hole, wall-mounted faucet, design by Philippe Starck as part
of the Axor Starck range □ **www.hansgrohe.com**

3 Cobra-Therm vertical, wall-fixed radiator in stainless steel, doubles
as a towel-warming rail □ **www.bisque.co.uk**

4 Plywood, countertop style of sink; also available by the same
manufacturer in the BluToo range are sinks in materials as diverse as
glass, stainless steel, cedarwood, and stone □ **www.minetti.de**

5 Stainless steel switches and outlets □ **www.forbesandlomax.co.uk**

6 An unusual and witty use of exterior decking material, to give this
bathroom the feel of a Japanese bathhouse. The wood is massanduba
□ **for wooden decking, see the Directory of Suppliers on pages 152–55**

7 The clever device of sinking the bath just slightly below floor level
is unexpected and magically adds to the air of luxury. It is a Jazz Solo,
steel inset design □ **www.duravit.com**

8 A single-lever faucet designed by Philippe Starck as part of the Axor
Starck range □ **www.hansgrohe.com**

9 Chinese sea grass floor covering. The sea grass is latex backed and
also available in herringbone design □ **for natural floor coverings, see
the Directory of Suppliers on pages 152–55**

Trumpet (2002) by Jorrit Kortenhorst
□ **www.moooi.com**

Romeo Moon T1 (1998) by Philippe Starck
□ **www.flos.net**

One From The Heart (1989) by Ingo Maurer
□ **www.ingo-maurer.com**

Le Klint 102 by Tove & Edv Kindt-Larsen
□ **www.leklint.com**

Miss K (2003) by Philippe Starck
□ **www.flos.net**

Kaipo (2001) by Edward van Vliet
□ **www.moooi.com**

Shadows (1998) by Marcel Wanders
□ **www.cappellini.it**

Atollo (1977) by Vico Magistretti
□ **www.oluce.com**

Fiesta pendant lamp, Model No. PB12, in frosted white glass □ **www.radiant.co.za**

Silo table lamp, Model No. JF161, with linen shade □ **www.radiant.co.za**

Blurring the boundaries
by Marco Bezzoli, Michael Borgstrom, and Adi Goren at architecture dot com
email: marco.arch@absamail.co.za

The brief for this apartment on Cape Town's Atlantic seaboard was to maximize views over the coast and create interiors that are "earthy yet timeless." The building's design is a pared-down palette of stainless steel, wood, stone, and glass with a hint of sixties retro styling. The theme is carried through to the interiors with the use of the same materials. The interiors are finished primarily in the muted colors of the travertine tiling and off-white painted walls to dampen the sea glare. A key element of the design is the flexible open-plan interior; the feeling of spaciousness is further enhanced by the "floating" roof structure and its band of horizontal windows, which give a 360-degree view of the surrounding mountains, sky, and sea. The bedroom and bathroom flow together, with the shower behind the bed in a glass cubicle, from where bathers can enjoy the sea views.

1 Bathroom wall tiled in 100 x 400mm (4 x 15¾") unsealed beige Turkish travertine tiles, which were cut to size on site by the tiler □ **for tiles, see the Directory of Suppliers on pages 152–55**

2 Single-lever faucet tap in chrome from the Tower-Tech range by La Torre □ **www.latorre-spa.it**

3 Corri 1 cast marble-resin deep sink by Marble Cast □ **www.marblecast.co.za**

4 Built-in wardrobes in solid Australian jarrah wood, designed by architecture dot com □ **e-mail: marco.arch@absamail.co.za**

5 Float 01 bed in solid Australian jarrah wood designed by architecture dot com □ **e-mail: marco.arch@absamail.co.za**

6 Floor tiled in 600 x 600mm (23½") honed and filled, vein-cut Turkish travertine tiles □ **for tiles, see the Directory of Suppliers on pages 152–55**

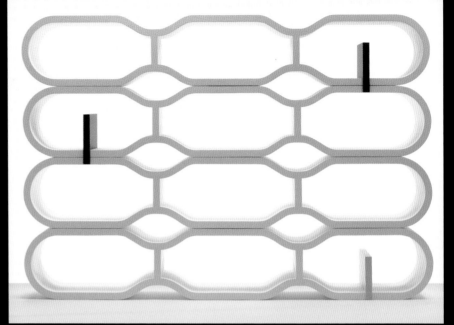

Brick by Ronan & Erwan Bouroullec
□ **www.cappellini.it**

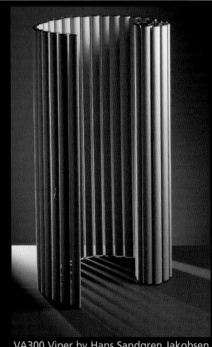

Extendable Screen (2004) by Tom Dixon
□ **www.tomdixon.net**

LA150 Labyrint by Pelikan Design
□ **www.fritzhansen.com**

VA300 Viper by Hans Sandgren Jakobsen
□ **www.fritzhansen.com**

Screen Model No. 100 in natural lacquered pine
(1933–36), Alvar Aalto ▫ **www.artek.fi**

Stool Model No. 60 in birch with white linoleum seat
(1932–33), Alvar Aalto ▫ **www.artek.fi**

Rural retreat
by Knud Holscher
www.knudholscher.dk

This sleeping area forms part of an unusual open-plan summer retreat. It has been designed by internationally renowned architect and designer Knud Holscher, who has worked on projects from airports to the award-winning "d line" range of stainless-steel door furniture. The single-story building, used by Holscher as a vacation retreat, features a gentle barrel-vaulted roof and is wrapped around with floor-to-ceiling glass walls and doors. The only solid wall inside the building encloses the bathroom area. A contemporary take on the traditional Scandinavian vacation cabin, this structure uses a limited palette of simple materials—Danish fir is used inside and out, with sheet plywood to line the ceiling and fir for flooring. The rough-hewn square wooden posts were discovered in a salvage yard.

1 Birch ply sheeting, an inexpensive, entirely practical and good-looking solution to lining the curved ceiling. Ply sheeting is widely available from lumberyards ▫ **for wood, see the Directory of Suppliers on pages 152–55**

2 Extra-wide Venetian blinds have been custom made to fit in each window bay ▫ **for blinds, see the Directory of Suppliers on pages 152–55**

3 A Knud Holscher prototype bed design, which features a platform on oversized wheels, making it possible to move the bed to expand the living area. The bed also has a large padded, sliding headrest and two cantilevered shelves ▫ **www.knudholscher.dk**

4 Natural Danish fir floorboards given a translucent pale gray wash, which allows the pattern of the grain to show through ▫ **for wood flooring, see the Directory of Suppliers on pages 152–55**

LC4 (1928) by Le Corbusier, Jeanneret & Perriand
□ www.cassina.it

Atlantic (2002) by Mårten Claesson, Eero Koivisto & Ola Rune
□ www.dune-ny.com

PK80 (1957) by Poul Kjærholm
□ www.fritzhansen.com

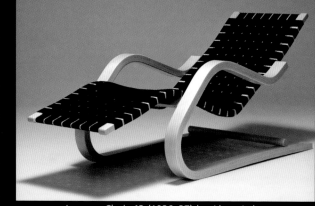

Lounge Chair 43 (1936–37) by Alvar Aalto
□ www.artek.fi

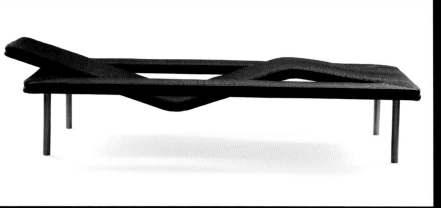

Oyster Daybed (1998) by Nigel Coates
□ www.lloydloom.com

Daybed (1925) by Eileen Gray
□ www.classicon.com

Le Klint 172 pendant lamp (1972),
Poul Christiansen □ **www.leklint.com**

Long Chair in birch (1935–36), Marcel Breuer
□ **www.isokonplus.com**

Best of both worlds
by Robert Dye at Robert Dye Associates
www.robertdye.com

This Regency-period townhouse was in poor
shape when it was brought by its current owners.
The architect's brief was to refurbish and restore
the place and make it fit for twenty-first-century
family life. Because the property is a registered
landmark, it was important to retain and repair
the period details; however, contemporary design
has also been integrated. After lengthy
negotiations with the local authority, it was
possible to add a modest glass extension at
garden level, and the designer owner has used
rooms as a showcase for her designs, including
wallpaper and lighting. The bedroom is an
example of where the Regency backdrop has
been retained, complete with picture rail and
original fireplace, and then contemporary
furniture and furnishings are added into the mix.

1 Wallpaper on wall and lampshade is Jocelyn
Warner's oversize pattern called Oval Shimmer from
the Totem range □ **www.jocelynwarner.com**

2 Oval Shimmer lampshade by Jocelyn Warner
□ **www.jocelynwarner.com**

3 Print above fireplace is by Sir Charles Wheeler

4 Peep bedside table from The Conran Shop
□ **www.conran.com**

5 Byron bed by Matthew Hilton. Solid maple framed
bed with veneered headboard; also available in
American cherry □ **www.scp.co.uk**

6 Wire-base occasional table (1950) by Charles and
Ray Eames □ **www.vitra.com**

7 A fresh look is achieved with simple white-painted
floorboards. Floor paint will look good for longer than
an ordinary gloss □ **for paint, including floor paint,
see the Directory of Suppliers on pages 152–55**

• A home office generates paperwork and other material; take stock of the shelving and cabinet space you need.

• Desk lamps prevent eyestrain and headaches, as well as improving concentration.

• A good chair is essential for day-to-day comfort and to avoid the debilitating effects of back pain. Look for ergonomic features, including adjustable, padded seat and armrests and casters.

• Working at home requires a substantial desk with a good size work space—an area of no less than 4 feet by 2 feet—set at a comfortable height.

• Plan shelving and cabinets for easy and immediate access to items you use every day; books or files used less often can be stored farther away.

• If possible, place your desk somewhere near a window; views and natural sunlight can be uplifting.

up commuting, canteens, and office gossip to work freelance, while those in regular employment are spending more and more time working at home. To ensure a productive and enjoyable experience, the home workspace has to be inviting and comfortable. Depending on the type of work, the is likely to be on an upper floor and therefore blessed with good natural light, and has the bonus of being separated from general family noise and disturbance. Where space is at a premium, think about setting up a desk in a regularly used bedroom where it will be quiet during the day.

WORK SPACES

space doesn't have to be enormous, but if you take your work seriously, it pays to make sure the office is well designed. For most people the mini-mum requirement will be a desk and chair with shelving and storage. The classic home office location is the guest bedroom, which makes excellent use of a room that is otherwise underused. If It might be worth considering an attic conversion or extension to gain valuable extra space. The desk and chair should be chosen with care—a large work surface is ideal and an office-style chair with ergonomic features will ensure that you avoid the perils and pains of back injury caused by sitting on inappropriate chairs.

Model No. S285 (1930–31) by Marcel Breuer
□ **www.thonet.de**

Model No. 2629, Radice (2001) by Roberto Barbieri
□ **www.zanotta.it**

Office System by System 180
□ **www.system180.de**

Model No. 465, Helsinki (1995) by
Caronni Bonanomi □ **www.desalto.it**

Model No. 2725, Comacina (1930) by Piero Bottoni
□ **www.zanotta.it**

Scrittarello (1997) by Achille Castiglioni
□ **www.depadova.it**

Loop Desk (1999) by Edward Barber & Jay Osgerby
□ **www.cappellini.it**

Nomos (1989) by Foster & Partners
□ **www.tecnospa.com**

Soft Pad ea 217–219 in black leather (1969),
Charles & Ray Eames □ www.vitra.com

Burdick Group modular office system (1980),
Bruce Burdick □ www.hermanmiller.com

2

1

3

Zen simplicity
by Ou Baholyodhin Studio
www.ou-b.com

A home office in the famous 1930s London apartment block Highpoint, owned by the designer Ou Baholyodhin. This room, part of a penthouse apartment, has remained largely unchanged since the apartments were designed and built by Berthold Lubetkin between 1935 and 1938. It is a calm and uncluttered office space, furnished with pieces of iconic furniture—the Eames-design Soft Pad chair is a widely acknowledged classic; the desk is by Bruce Burdick and forms part of the modular system called the Burdick Group. This is a modular system built around an interchangeable kit of parts, connected by aluminum beams and brackets, to support work surfaces, equipment, and storage elements.

1 An unusual, almost sculptural shelving design believed to have been designed by the apartment's original architect, Berthold Lubetkin □ **for office furniture, including shelving, see the Directory of Suppliers on pages 152–55**

2 An intriguing wall constructed from huge slices of Norwegian fir. The assertive texture of this wood has maximum impact when seen in such a controlled Modernist setting □ **www.nordictimber.org**

3 Earth-colored quarry tiles, a standard product available from all good tile retailers. The contrasting white grout picks out the grid pattern □ **for stone flooring, see the Directory of Suppliers on pages 152–55**

Aeron (1992) by Don Chadwick &
Bill Stumpf □ **www.hermanmiller.com**

Byrne (2000) by Eero Koivisto
□ **www.david.se**

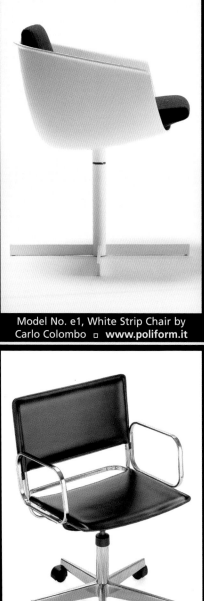

Polo Chair (1973) by Robin Day
□ **www.loftonline.net**

Model No. e1, White Strip Chair by
Carlo Colombo □ **www.poliform.it**

Soft Pad (1969) by Charles & Ray Eames
□ **www.hermanmiller.com**

Model No. 5263, Flow (2000) by
Burkhardt Vogtherr □ **www.fritzhansen.com**

Model No. 3271, Oxford (1965) by
Arne Jacobsen □ **www.fritzhansen.com**

Model No. 3117, Series 7 (1955) by
Arne Jacobsen □ **www.fritzhansen.com**

Model No. 2290, Cassia (1974) by De Pas,
D'Urbino & Lomazzi □ **www.zanotta.it**

Tizio desk lamp (1972), Richard Sapper
□ **www.artemide.com**

Kevi office chair (1974), Jørgen Rasmussen
□ **www.fritzhansen.com**

The pleasures of high office
by Grut Partnership &
Toh Shimazaki Architecture
email: lg@dial.pipex.com □ www.t-sa.co.uk

Raised up on the second floor of this family house, the work space occupies pride of place at the south-facing rear of the building with views across the local park. A small extension has provided the room with a glassy roof and full-height doors, which lead to the sunny terrace. One of the owners is an architect and works at home full time; the other is an engineer, working at home some of the time. Because they spend so much of their working lives here, a good-quality space was essential. In addition to a comfortable working environment, a generous-sized work surface and well-ordered storage space are essentials.

1 Tolomeo aluminum wall lamp (1987) by Michele de Lucchi and Giancarlo Fassina □ **www.artemide.com**

2 606 Universal Shelving System (1960) by Dieter Rams. A timeless, strong, handsome modular system, which along with shelving, comprises filing drawers, cabinets, and worktops. □ **www.vitsoe.com**

3 Tall, slim, wall-fixed radiators. The color was specially requested by the client □ **www.hudevad.com**

4 An elongated D-shaped table with ash top finished in pale gray linoleum, customized by the architect, Ann Grut. Circular and rectangular tables in birch are produced by Artek □ **www.artek.fi**

5 Flooring is a gray wool carpet □ **for carpet, see the Directory of Suppliers on pages 152–55**

6 Wastepaper basket in metal mesh □ **www.ikea.com**

LC7 Swivel Chair (1928) by Le Corbusier, Jeanneret & Perriand □ **www.cassina.it**

Comet by Team Johanson □ **www.johansondesign.se**

Felt Chair (1994) by Marc Newson □ **www.cappellini.it**

Sax Mini (2004) by Terence Woodgate □ **www.scp.co.uk**

Spanish Chair (1958) by Børge Mogensen □ **www.fredericia.com**

Revolt (1953) by Friso Kramer □ **www.ahrend.com**

Thinking Man's Chair (1987) by Jasper Morrison □ **www.cappellini.it**

Model No. CH25 (1950) by Hans J. Wegner □ **www.carlhansen.com**

LCP (Low Chair Plastic) (1996) by Mårten van Severen □ **www.kartell.it**

Hi-Pad (1999) by Jasper Morrison □ **www.cappellini.it**

Model No. D80 (1982) by Axel Bruchhäuser after Jean Prouvé □ **www.tecta.de**

DCM (1946), Charles & Ray Eames from Herman Miller, also available □ **www.vitra.com**

Fiberglass Chair (1948–50), Charles & Ray Eames, from Herman Miller, reissued as Plastic Chair □ **www.vitra.com**

Library of the future
by Francine Houben at Mecanoo
www.mecanoo.com

With its far-reaching canal views, this top-floor library is a place for quiet contemplation and research. The new home sits at the end of a row of nineteenth-century houses and is planned with living space on the upper first floor, and bedrooms and the library above. It is a house without halls and corridors and is designed with all living areas as a sequence of continuous flowing space. As this picture shows, the upper library level is linked visually to the lower living room by the use of a void by the open staircase. The threshold to the library is marked subtly in the change of flooring. The house combines stone, concrete, glass, steel, and wood, solid and soft, simple and precious, in a complete composition.

1 Abstracta shelving system, designed in the 1970s by Danish architect Poul Cadovius. Abstracta is a space frame and store fixture system noted for its stability and versatility □ **www.abstracta.com**

2 Afzelia wood flooring. An extremely hard-wearing African-grown wood, which possesses the durability of teak, the hardness of oak, and the look of iroko □ **for wood flooring, see the Directory of Suppliers on pages 152–55**

3 Zebra pattern rug. For designer collections see □ **www.designercarpets.com**

Componibili (1967–69) by Anna Castelli Ferrieri
□ **www.kartell.it**

Kitos Modular Office System by USM
□ **www.usm.com**

Model No. 740/50, Soho (2001–02) by
Emaf Progetti □ **www.zanotta.it**

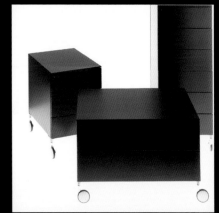

Roller I, II, III by Marco Zanuso Jr.
□ **www.driade.com**

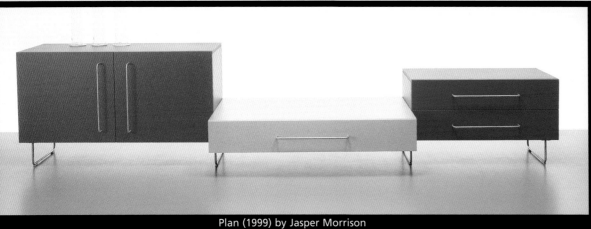

Plan (1999) by Jasper Morrison
□ **www.cappellini.it**

Mobil (1994) by Antonio Citterio & Glen Oliver Löw
□ **www.kartell.it**

Hard-working space
by Rainer Spehl

www.rainerspehl.com

Plenty of storage space and easy access to files, reference, and papers formed the brief for this home office design. The owner works in marketing and needed to have rapid access to information while sitting at the desk. The designer Rainer Spehl is first and foremost a furniture designer, and for his interior projects, including this office, he creates installations like large pieces of furniture. One of his trademarks is to reuse existing materials and incorporate them in his furniture. A warm-colored backdrop for the desk was formed with sheet oak veneer; the desk top is built in, also using oak. The shelves above were made with off-the-rail brackets and MDF shelving painted olive green—a nosing at the front of the shelf hides the brackets. A custom-designed drawer cabinet on wheels was made to fit under the desktop. The closed cabinet wall provides storage space for items less frequently in use.

1 A wall of tall cabinets provides capacious storage space for filing and paperwork associated with the client's job. It is used for items needed regularly but not daily. Long steel handles add a touch of elegance. Long cabinet handles in a number of designs and made in satin stainless steel are available from various manufacturers, including d line ▫ **www.dline.com** ▫ FSB ▫ **www.fsb.de** ▫ and Allgood plc ▫ **www.allgood.co.uk**

2 Simple shelving kit from a regular hardware store. The planks of olive-green-painted MDF rest on standard wall brackets. A nosing has been fixed to the front of the shelves to obscure the brackets ▫ **for office furniture, including shelving, see the Directory of Suppliers on pages 152–55**

3 Tizio desk lamp (1972) by Richard Sapper. This lamp is the epitome of matte-black cool from the 1970s, a beautifully balanced, elegant desk lamp, also available as a floor lamp ▫ **www.artemide.com**

4 Pine board flooring, which has been given a matte lacquer finish ▫ **for wood flooring, see the Directory of Suppliers on pages 152–55**

.04 office chair with flexible polyurethane foam shell, Mårten van Severen ▫ **www.vitra.com**

Custom-made desk and drawer unit, Rainer Spehl ▫ **www.rainerspehl.com**

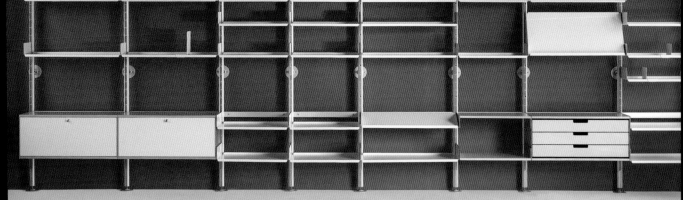

606 Universal Shelving System (1960) by Dieter Rams
□ **www.vitsoe.com**

Model No. 731, Ulm (1996–98) by
Enzo Mari □ **www.zanotta.it**

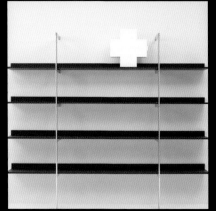

Aliante by Giulio Cappellini &
Rodolfo Dordoni □ **www.cappellini.it**

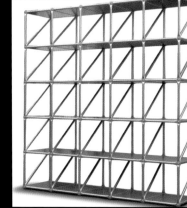

Office System by System 180
□ **www.system180.de**

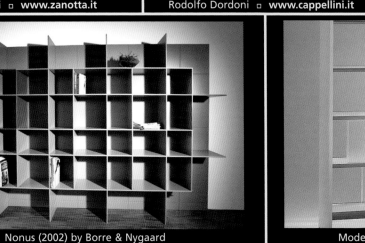

Nonus (2002) by Borre & Nygaard
□ **www.nordictrend.com**

Model No. 346, Raster (2001) by Jorge Pensi
□ **www.cassina.it**

Bookworm (1994) by Ron Arad
□ **www.kartell.it**

Model No. 114 Nuvola Rossa (1977) by
Vico Magistretti □ **www.cassina.it**

Speaking volumes

by Augustin + Frank Architekten

www.augustinundfrank.de

This elegant workroom with a view was created in the new-build, contemporary home designed for an antiquarian bookseller. One of the main requirements for the office was plenty of shelving to house the massive collection of books. The house was built incorporating sturdy concrete to withstand the tremendous weight of books. The vast window was constructed to introduce plenty of natural light and give fantastic, uninterrupted views over the wooded garden.

1 Lighting raft suspended over the desk to ensure good-quality light for working. It is impossible to overestimate the important of good lighting while at work; it prevents eyestrain and headaches and aids concentration. Many companies produce specialist office lighting, including Light Corporation □ **www.lightcorp.com** □ Erco □ **www.erco.com** □ and Louis Poulsen □ **www.louis-poulsen.com**

2 Modular shelving system to provide maximum storage space can be extended when more space is required. Low-level shelves in the same black-stained wood complement the bookcases. For smart contemporary systems, see Aviolux and Archi from Cappellini □ **www.cappellini.it** □ Spatio Office by Antonio Citterio and Glen Oliver Löw □ **www.vitra.com** □ and the rigorous Oikos (1998) and Kaos (1986) systems by Antonia Astori □ **www.driade.com**

3 A blond wood table makes a simple desk with generous-size work surface. For great classic office furniture see the Knoll office systems and Knoll Studio ranges □ **www.knollint.com**

4 A spectacular feature of the house is this wall of glass. It was custom made by Gretsch-Unitas □ **www.g-u.de**

5 An industrial-quality oak floor, the type of hard-wearing material you might find in a car showroom or store □ **for wood flooring, see the Directory of Suppliers on pages 152–55**

Archimoon Tech (1998) by Philippe Starck
□ www.flos.net

AJ (1957–60) by Arne Jacobsen
□ www.louis-poulsen.com

Table Lamp BS712 (1969) by Ben af Schulten
□ www.artek.fi

Arà (1988) by Philippe Starck
□ www.flos.net

Snoopy (1967) by Achille &
Pier Giacomo Castiglioni □ www.flos.net

Bulb (1966) by Ingo Maurer
□ www.ingo-maurer.com

RHa (1981–84) by Dieter Rams &
Andreas Hackbarth □ www.tecnolumen.de

Type 3 (2003) by Herbert Terry & Sons
□ www.anglepoise.com

606 Universal Shelving System (1960), Dieter Rams □ **www.vitsoe.com**

Oskar lamp (1998), Ingo Maurer □ **www.ingo-maurer.com**

High Frame chair in aluminum, Alberto Meda □ **www.aliasdesign.it**

Shelf life
by Design Service at Vitsoe

www.vitsoe.com

The refurbishment of this 1960s home included opening up the entire ground floor by removing the entrance hall and its eight doors, which led to various parts of the living space. A new work area was designed to fit in the previously unused space under the original stairs. On the other side of this wall is the kitchen. The classic Vitsoe 606 Universal Shelving System was used to construct the office area; part of it is wall fixed

and part is fixed between floor and ceiling, where it extends beyond the end of the wall toward the dining area. A comprehensive modular system, it is constructed in aluminum, steel, wood, and laminate. The wall comprises shelving, a three-drawer cabinet, three one-drawer cabinets, and a small integrated laminate table. At the far end, the reverse side of the system is used for storing flatware, linens, and glasses. The use of wide-board oak flooring throughout visually ties the spaces together. For continuity, an Alberto Meda-designed High Frame chair is used at the desk, as well as at the table for a dining chair.

1 The original 1960s stairs have been refurbished and the center part of the tread wrapped in leather □ **for furnishings, fabrics, and textiles, including leather, see the Directory of Suppliers on pages 152–55**

2 Costanza pendant lamp (1985) by Paolo Rizzatto. Also available as a floor, table, and wall lamp with a square natural aluminum, black, or iron-gray stand. The silk-screen printed polycarbonate shade is available in a range of colors □ **www.luceplan.com**

3 Vitsoe dining table, which is no longer in production and is now a collector's item □ **for vintage furniture, see the Directory of Suppliers on pages 152–55**

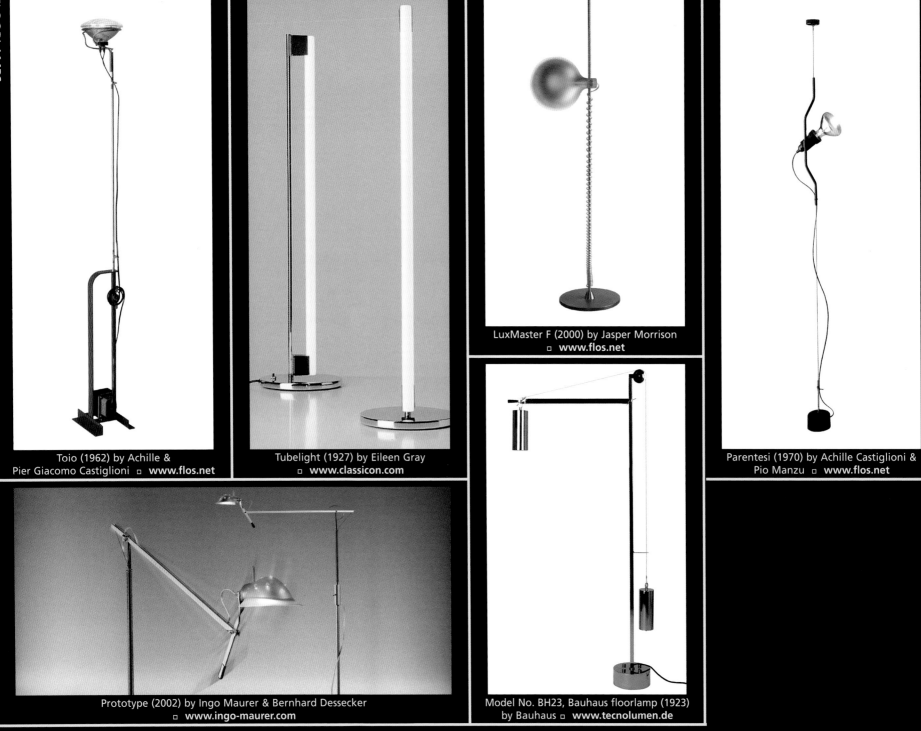

Toio (1962) by Achille &
Pier Giacomo Castiglioni □ **www.flos.net**

Tubelight (1927) by Eileen Gray
□ **www.classicon.com**

LuxMaster F (2000) by Jasper Morrison
□ **www.flos.net**

Parentesi (1970) by Achille Castiglioni &
Pio Manzu □ **www.flos.net**

Prototype (2002) by Ingo Maurer & Bernhard Dessecker
□ **www.ingo-maurer.com**

Model No. BH23, Bauhaus floorlamp (1923)
by Bauhaus □ **www.tecnolumen.de**

Trapeze low-voltage track lighting system
□ **www.mr-resistor.co.uk**

Soft Pad ea 217–219 in black leather (1969),
Charles & Ray Eames □ **www.vitra.com**

Fertile imagination
by Mary Manatiy at
Marston Manatiy Design
www.marstonmanatiydesign.com

As part of the refurbishment of an elegant
nineteenth-century London riverside apartment,
the former Japanese-style sunroom has been
cleverly converted for use as a home office. It
sits on the third floor of the building and has
magnificent views. To help protect the interior
from overheating in full sunlight, floor-to-ceiling
blinds have been fitted around the whole interior.
To maximize enjoyment of, and to reflect, the
cityscape, the natural light, and the constantly
moving river, the refurbishment of the home has
included a liberal use of clear and colored glass
and mirrors.

1 An antique triple-stem globe lamp from the 1960s,
a secondhand find. The lamp is reminiscent of the great
Arco of 1962 by Achille and Pier Giacomo Castiglioni,
for Flos □ **www.flos.net**

2 Cedar floral wood-slat Venetian blinds
□ **for blinds, see the Directory of Suppliers on
pages 152–55**

3 1930s-style steel desk by Müller, part of the Classic
Line range of office furniture
□ **www.mueller-moebel.com**

4 American oak, engineered planks with oiled finish
□ **for wood flooring, see the Directory of Suppliers on
pages 152–55**

5 Tan leather storage box
□ **www.theholdingcompany.co.uk**

Model. No. T0521, Butterfly Stool (1956) by
Sori Yanagi □ **www.tendo-mokko.co.jp**

Model No. EJ 144 by Anne Mette Jensen &
Morten Ernst □ **www.erik-joergensen.com**

Jakkara by Durat
□ **www.durat.com**

Corks (2002) by Jasper Morrison
□ **www.moooi.com**

La Bohème (2001) by Philippe Starck
□ **www.kartell.it**

Time-Life Stool (1960) by Charles &
Ray Eames □ **www.vitra.com**

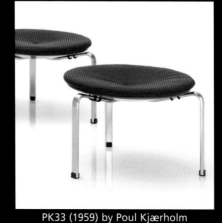

PK33 (1959) by Poul Kjærholm
□ **www.fritzhansen.com**

18 inch polished stool (2002) by
Philippe Starck □ **www.emeco.net**

Model No. 220, Mezzadro (1957) by
Achille Castiglioni □ **www.zanotta.it**

Table Lamp BS712 (1969),
Ben af Schulten □ www.artek.fi

Stool Model No. 60 in birch with red linoleum seat
(1932–33), Alvar Aalto □ www.artek.fi

Rest, work, and play
by Haroma Partners
www.haromapartners.fi

With an enviable position on the banks of a river, this brick-built former school building has now been converted into simple, loft-style apartments. A double-height space at the window end of the rectangular apartment is used for the dining and sitting areas. Toward the back is a mezzanine floor, underneath which is the kitchen and bathroom, while above is this open-plan bedroom and home office. A unifying factor in this simple interior is the choice of furniture all from the same family, made in birch wood and designed by Finnish architect Alvar Aalto (1898–1976), who set up his own company, Artek, to manufacturer his designs.

1 Zebra pattern rug. For designer collections see □ **www.designercarpets.com**

2 A daybed called 710 was designed by Alvar Aalto and remains in production. Meanwhile another of his bed designs based on a steel tube frame is made by Wohnbedarf Basel □ **www.wohnbedarf.com**

3 Table 80A (1933–35) by Alvar Aalto. A birch wood table, which doubles as a desk, with red linoleum surface □ **www.artek.fi**

4 Chair 611 (1929–30) by Alvar Aalto. A stackable, birch wood chair with black webbing upholstery. Also available with leather seating □ **www.artek.fi**

5 Pedestal 297 (1929–30) by Alvar Aalto. A birch wood stack of five shallow drawers, which can rest on a plinth, as shown here, or be fitted with casters □ **www.artek.fi**

• To make a small outside space appear larger, add a sculpture or water feature to the farthest wall to draw the eye through the space; when illuminated at night, it will look particularly impressive.

• A small toolshed or storage box is always useful for stowing away any extra cushions, rugs, candles, deck chairs, and a few garden tools.

• Mirrors fixed to walls create the illusion of extra space.

• Garden lighting can be magical—use spotlights to illuminate trees or Christmas tree lights around a dining area; keep light levels low to avoid annoying neighbors.

• A table and chairs are essential for making a social space—opt for the luxury of teak or the practicality of materials like aluminum that can be left outside.

• An outdoor sound system is a real luxury.

Gardens and yards not only look different from the way they did a few years ago; they are also being used in other ways. Traditional lawns with perennial borders have given way to low-maintenance gardens. You don't need a huge space to enjoy being outside; even the smallest balcony or terrace can be colonized

menus and to let your imagination run wild. Be frivolous or outrageous in your designs. Just as you would decorate a room, think about flooring materials and color schemes and the style of furniture and lighting. There is also the opportunity to add extra interest, perhaps with a water feature, to expand the sense of space with

OUTDOOR SPACES

with a table, chairs, and potted plants. The garden has become an extension of the interior, and in many homes, the main living room now leads on to the garden through sliding or folding doors, which blur the boundaries between inside and out. An outdoor room should be used as often as possible; it is a place to entertain family and

mirrors, or to add a sculpture in the distance to draw the eye through the space. To help achieve the desired effect, designers and manufacturers are producing ranges of beautiful outdoor furniture, interesting decking and paving materials, sophisticated barbecues and ovens, and excellent outdoor lighting.

Arne Jacobsen Seat by Arne Jacobsen
▫ **www.listerteak.com**

Urban Garden Bench by Matthew Hilton
▫ **www.scp.co.uk**

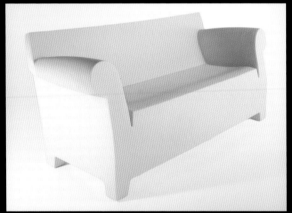

Bubble Club (2000) by Philippe Starck
▫ **www.kartell.it**

Phantom (2004) by Peter Emrys-Roberts
▫ **www.driade.com**

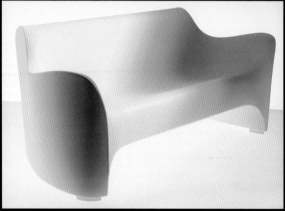

Tokyo-Pop (2002) by Tokujin Yoshioka
▫ **www.kartell.it**

Model No. 980, Camilla (1984) by
Castiglioni & Pozzi ▫ **www.zanotta.it**

Haven by Barlow Tyrie
▫ **www.barlowtyrie.com**

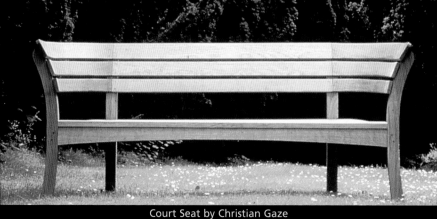

Court Seat by Christian Gaze
▫ **www.gazeburvill.com**

No Limit table with zinc-covered extending end for planters, Kerstin Olby ▢ www.olbydesign.se

Element aluminum wall lights, Kina Strandberg & Marie Lundgren ▢ www.smakdesign.se

String lounger in pine, Kerstin Olby ▢ www.olbydesign.se

Sun, moon, and stars
Nina Thalinson at Lust & Fägring
www.lustochfagring.se

Even the smallest garden becomes a beautiful and welcoming place with ingenious lighting and appealing materials. This urban design is conceived as an extension to the house and as a place to enjoy the sun, as well as the stars in the nighttime sky. The pergola makes a framework for the dining space, furnished with table and stools. The net of tiny lights guarantees a romantic starry evening even when it is cloudy.

1 The pergola is constructed from steel beams covered with a net studded with tiny low-voltage bulbs. The frame acts a climbing support for Humulus Japonicus, an ornamental vine also known as the Japanese hop ▢ **for lighting, see the Directory of Suppliers on pages 152–55**

2 The waterfall feature is made of glass blocks set in a steel frame. A pump ensures steady and slow trickles of water down the face of the glass blocks. A sheet of aluminum foil has been fixed to the wall behind the bricks to act as a reflector for the light from a pair of lamps, also fixed behind the blocks. There is a 2-inch gap between wall and glass blocks ▢ **www.lustochfagring.se**

3 Plant pots made of sand-cast recycled aluminum from Byarums Bruk ▢ **www.byarumsbruk.se**

4 Pall Lilla Li stools with rope seats by Kerstin Olby ▢ **www.olbydesign.se**

5 Big concrete pots with glass staves for climbing plants, designed by Nina Thalinson and Eva Paradis, handmade at the Paradis Workshop ▢ **www.paradisverstaden.se**

6 Gray paving bricks, framed by concrete paving of larger pinkish bricks with a flower relief pattern, designed by Cissa Sundling ▢ **www.lustochfagring.se**

Broadway Round Table by Lister Teak
□ **www.listerteak.com**

FOG Table (1999) by Frank O. Gehry
□ **www.knoll.com**

MR Side Table (1927–29) by Ludwig
Mies van der Rohe □ **www.knoll.com**

Model No. C4 A-D, Nesting Tables (1925–26)
by Marcel Breuer □ **www.tecta.de**

Equinox by Barlow Tyrie
□ **www.barlowtyrie.com**

Windsor by Barlow Tyrie
□ **www.barlowtyrie.com**

Bubu (1996) by Philippe Starck
□ **www.xo-design.com**

Model No. 2830, Quaderna (1970) by Superstudio
□ **www.zanotta.it**

Dining table with zinc top, Stephen Woodhams
□ **www.woodhams.co.uk**

Dining out in the urban jungle
Stephen Woodhams at Woodhams
www.woodhams.co.uk

Rising from the urban jungle is this African-themed roof terrace, which sits on the nineteenth floor and has spectacular city-wide views. The design is conceived as an extension of the apartment interior below, which incorporates many of the same materials, colors, and textures. The unusual herringbone pattern terrace might usually be built in brick, but here has been laid like a parquet flooring and is made using three types of wood, iroko being prominent. The handsome dining table is completed with a pair of thronelike chairs, and beside this is a small sculpture garden where the lead sculptures are reminiscent of the shapes of spears and shields. Views are made possible even when seated, through the addition of glass panel balustrading.

1 A mixture of plants has been chosen; grasses include *Carex bucchanii* mixed with *Astelia chathamica* 'Silver Spear' and bamboo □ **www.woodhams.co.uk**

2 Zinc sculptures in shapes reminiscent of spears and shields by Sean Brosnan □ **www.woodhams.co.uk**

3 Planters add their own sculptural quality to the space, and are available in a wide range of materials □ **for garden furniture, see the Directory of Suppliers on pages 152–55**

4 Throne chairs in oak with brushed stainless steel-clad backs, custom design by Stephen Woodhams □ **www.woodhams.co.uk**

5 A herringbone-wood pattern floor made in wood, predominantly iroko □ **for wooden decking, see the Directory of Suppliers on pages 152–55**

Gwapa (2001) by Marcel Wanders
□ **www.moooi.com**

Model No. 2068, Mirandolina (1992) by
Pietro Arosio □ **www.zanotta.it**

Model No. 2076, Zilli (2002) by
Roberto Barbieri □ **www.zanotta.it**

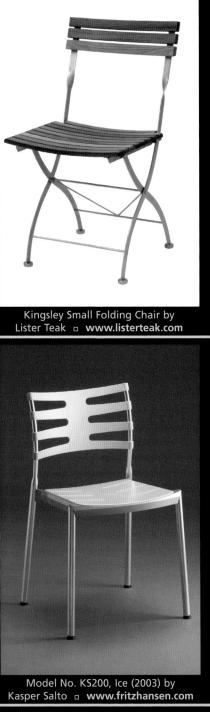

Kingsley Small Folding Chair by
Lister Teak □ **www.listerteak.com**

Model No. KS200, Ice (2003) by
Kasper Salto □ **www.fritzhansen.com**

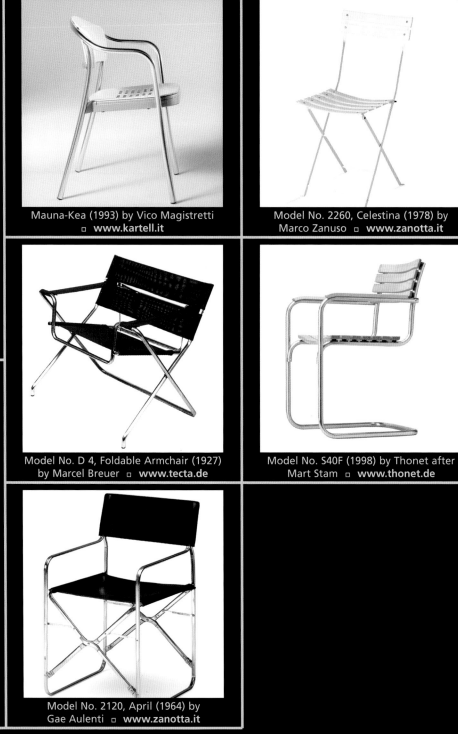

Mauna-Kea (1993) by Vico Magistretti
□ **www.kartell.it**

Model No. 2260, Celestina (1978) by
Marco Zanuso □ **www.zanotta.it**

Model No. D 4, Foldable Armchair (1927)
by Marcel Breuer □ **www.tecta.de**

Model No. S40F (1998) by Thonet after
Mart Stam □ **www.thonet.de**

Model No. 2120, April (1964) by
Gae Aulenti □ **www.zanotta.it**

Slick-Slick stackable chair in polypropylene (1999), Philippe Starck □ **www.xo-design.com**

Thali table in anodized aluminum with slatted top, Miki Astori □ **www.driade.com**

Less work and more play
Karena Batstone at Karena Batstone Design & Helen Tindale at Reversed Out
www.karenabatstone.com □

www.reversedout.com

The owners of this long town garden wanted a space that was easy to maintain, a place for entertaining and enjoying food outside, and a safe area for their child to play. The designers began by raising the level of the garden—it had been accessed from the basement level, but raising it made it much more easily accessed from the first floor. There are now steps up from the basement. A dining area was created using stone paving—this was pushed away from the house, to encourage better use of the garden. It also means that grown-ups can keep a close watch on playing children. A "secret" play area has been created at the far end of the garden behind the large wall of opal acrylic sheeting.

1 Opal colored acrylic sheet □ **for plastics, see the Directory of Suppliers on pages 152–55**

2 Stainless-steel planters made by specialist metalworker □ **www.elitemetalcraft.co.uk**

3 Stone paving supplied by the client. It is vital to select a stone that is appropriate for the location. Where frost is likely to occur, a natural frost-resistant material such as sandstone is a good idea. Ceramic tiles may also be used, as well as slate and marble. Check with your supplier □ **for stone paving, see the Directory of Suppliers on pages 152–55**

4 Lighting has been carefully located around the garden and includes uplighters to illuminate the pretty silver birch trees □ **for suppliers of lighting see page 152 of the Directory**

5 Slate chips are used to create the path and boundary between dining area and grass □ **for stone paving, see the Directory of Suppliers on pages 152–55**

Safari Chair (1933) by Kaare Klint
▫ **www.rudrasmussen.dk**

Lord Yo (1994) by Philippe Starck
▫ **www.driade.com**

Haven Armchair with Ottoman by Barlow Tyrie
▫ **www.barlowtyrie**

Flower Chair (2001) by Marcel Wanders
▫ **www.moooi.com**

Dalai Daybed by Hyacinth
▫ **www.hyacinth-design.com**

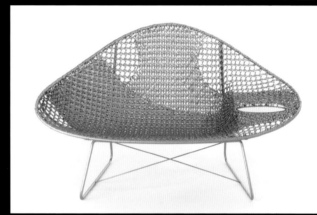

Lovenet (2002) by Ross Lovegrove
▫ **www.moooi.com**

KAAT Armchair by Wilfried Hendriks &
Steven Stals ▫ **www.listerteak.com**

Nemo (2003) by Jane Dillon & Tom Grieves
▫ **www.lloydloom.com**

Throw-away (1965) by Willie Landels
▫ **www.zanotta.it**

The pleasure garden
by Candy and Candy
www.candyandcandy.com

With growing numbers of city and town dwellers wanting to enjoy some outside space, there has been a tremendous growth in roof gardens. Even the very smallest of spaces can be transformed into a private terrace. Here among the chimney pots, a tiny terrace has been given an exotic Middle Eastern theme with the wood-frame daybed and a pair of extremely comfortable upholstered armchairs. A mirror is cleverly positioned to introduce reflections, which enhance the sense of space in this compact area. A sculpture and candlesticks are decorative accessories. The slow-growing hedge provides a natural screen from the homes on the opposite side of the road.

1 Custom-made simple daybed by Candy and Candy, which fits into the niche beside the chimney pots. It has been designed so that the canvas top is easily removed and stowed away with the cushions to protect them from the weather □ **www.candyandcandy.com**

2 Privacy is secured with this slow-growing hedge, which provides a natural screen from the homes opposite □ **for garden plants, see the Directory of Suppliers on pages 152–55**

3 Cedar wood decking, which is tough and durable. The grooved surface helps to prevent slipping □ **for wooden decking, see the Directory of Suppliers on pages 152–55**

4 Floor recessed lights add an extra dimension to this terrace, making it welcoming at night □ **for lighting, see the Directory of Suppliers on pages 152–55**

Upholstered armchair; for similar see Haven from Barlow Tyrie □ www.barlowtyrie.com

Natal Chaise Longue by Wim Segers
□ **www.tribu.be**

S Line Lounger by Lister Teak
□ **www.listerteak.com**

PK24 (1965) by Poul Kjærholm
□ **www.fritzhansen.com**

Seagull Lounger by Lister Teak
□ **www.listerteak.com**

Bowline Lounger (2004) by Gaze Burvill
□ **www.gazeburvill.com**

Model No. 930, Soft (1999) by Werner Aisslinger
□ **www.zanotta.it**

Lounger Model No. 5090, Lister Teak
☐ **www.listerteak.com**

Town garden
by The Plant Room
www.plantroom.co.uk

The owners of this town garden wanted a space for resting and entertaining that would involve minimal maintenance. The design is cleverly based on the diagonal across the long, but narrow garden, which makes an eye-catching layout and enhances the sense of space. Decking is set at different levels to landscape the area and break it into distinct spaces for sunbathing or dining. Planting, in ground level and raised beds, is designed to require as little maintenance as possible, and plants are set in small beds mulched with white cockleshells, which reflect the light and add textural interest. There is also a built-in irrigation system and wiring for outdoor lighting

1 Custom-made triangular shed designed by The Plant Room to fit into this corner of the garden. It provides valuable storage space for cushions, outdoor lights and candles, a minimal number of garden tools, and a brush for sweeping the decking ☐ **www.plantroom.co.uk**

2 An extremely clever and space-efficient way of achieving outdoor seating, this uses part of the blue-painted, blockwork retaining wall as an L-shaped seat to wrap around a large custom-made limestone-topped table. Although this is a small area, it can comfortably seat up to ten people ☐ **www.plantroom.co.uk**

3 A contemporary pergola built using wooden posts and regular copper piping from a building contracters' supplier. It provides the structure for this ancient Italian vine to clamber over ☐ **www.plantroom.co.uk**

4 To keep the budget down on this particular project, softwood decking was chosen. It is set at different levels to landscape the area and break it into distinct spaces. Another way of subtly separating the areas has been to lay the boards on each level at 90 degrees to the adjoining deck. Decking is widely available; all garden designers and good retailers will offer advice on what to choose ☐ **for wooden decking, see the Directory of Suppliers on pages 152–55**

Directory of suppliers

Associations and industry bodies

The American Institute of Architects
1735 New York Avenue NW,
Washington, DC 20006-5292
202-626-7300
www.aia.org

Association of Woodworking and Furniture Suppliers
5733 Rickenbacker Road,
Commerce, CA 90040
323-838-9440
www.awfs.org

Forest Stewardship Council U.S.
1155 30th Street NW, Suite 300,
Washington, DC 20007
202-342-0413
www.fscus.org
International body that certificates sustainable timber

National Association of Home Builders
1201 15th Street NW,
Washington, DC 20005
202-266-8400
www.nahb.org

Stone Network
e-mail: info@stone-network.com
www.stone-network.com
General information on stone. Includes a list of manufacturers and distributors of natural stone products thoughout the US

Sustainable Architecture, Building, and Culture
P.O. Box 30085,
Santa Barbara, CA 93130
323-838-9440
www.sustainbaleabc.com

Aquariums and fish tanks

Aquarium Designs
21 Madison Court,
Tinton Falls, NJ 07712
732-695-0986
www.aquariumdesigns.com

Aquatic Design Systems
6970 Convoy Court,
San Diego, CA 92111
858-636-7990

Crystal Clear Aquarium Services
301 9th Avenue,
Brunswick, MD 21716
301-834-8930
www.crysyalclearaquariums.com

Architectural glass

Loewen
77 Highway 52 West,
Steinbach, MB Canada
R5G 1B2
800-563-9367
www.loewen.com
Custom-made windows

NanaWall Systems, Inc.
707 Redwood Highway,
Mill Valley, CA 94941
800-873-5673
www.nanawall.com
Opening glass walls

Architectural salvage

American Salvage
9200 North West 27th Avenue,
Miami, FL 33147
305-691-7001
www.americansalvage.com
Recycled building materials, period architectural features, and household items

Whole House Building Supply
731-D Loma Verde Avenue,
Palo Alto, CA 94303-4161
650-856-0634
www.driftwoodsalvage.com
Salvaged wood and other items

Bathroom furniture and fixtures

Diamond Spas, Inc.
760 South 104th Street,
Broomfield, CO 80020
303-665-8303 / 800-951-7727
www.diamondspas.com
Custom-made contemporary bath fixtures made from stainless steel or copper, including modern Japanese-style soaking baths and showerpans

Duravit USA, Inc.
1750 Breckinridge Pakway, Suite 500,
Duluth, GA 30096
770-931-3575
www.duravit.com

European Home
307 Porter Street,
Melrose, MA 02176
781-662-1110
www.europeanhome.com
Contemporary bath fixtures, including Durat

Hansgrohe, Inc.
1490 Bluegrass Lakes Parkway,
Alpharetta, GA 30004
800-488-8119
www.hanghroe-usa.com

Lefroy Brooks USA
10 Leonard Street, Suite 2N
New York, NY10013
212-226-2242
www.lefroybrooks.com
Traditional and modern designs

ThermaSol
2255 Union Place,
Simi Valley, CA 93065
805-776-071
www.thermasol.com
Steam baths, saunas, fog-free mirrors. East-Coast branch details available on-line

TOTO USA, Inc.
1155 Southern Road,
Morrow, Georgia 30260
770-282-8686
www.totousa.com

Concrete flooring, sinks, and countertops

American Concrete Institute
P.O. Box 9094,
Farmington Hills, MI 48333
248-848-3700
www.aci-int.org
General information on concrete. List of manufacturers and distributors throughout the US

A to Z Precast Concrete Products, Inc.
4451 8th Avenue South,
St Petersburg, FL 33711
800-345-7821
www.atozprecast.com
Wide range of concrete products available including precast concrete decking, fencing, and custom-made building elements

Operative Plasterers' and Cement Masons' International Association (OPCMIA)
14405 Laurel Place, Suite 300,
Laurel, ML 20707
301-470-4200
www.opcmia.org
General information on concrete. List of recommended masons throughout the US

Carpets and rugs

ABC Carpet and Home
888 Broadway @ East 19th Street,
New York, NY 10003
212-473-3000
www.abchome.com

Christopher Farr USA, Inc.
748 North La Cienega Boulevard
Los Angeles, CA 90069
310-967-0064
www.christopherfarr.com

Current Carpets Gallery
Cypress Village, P.O. Box 1127,
39138 Ocean Drive C6-2,
Gualala, CA 95445
800-485-8980
www.currentcarpets.com
Contemporary wool carpets

Natural Area Rugs, Inc.
8306 Wilshire Boulevard # 4500,
Beverly Hills, CA 90211
323-233-6666
www.naturalarearugs.com
Manufacturer and importer of natural rugs and carpets. Range includes sisal, seagrass, mountain grass, and jute rugs and carpets

Roger Oates Design
Y & Co.
247 Davenport Road, Suite 301,
Toronto, Ontario M5R 1J9
416-968-7700
www.rogeroates.com
Handmade rugs in wool, linen, or cotton

The Rug Company
88 Wooster Street,
New York, NY 10012
212-274-0444
8202 Melrose Avenue,
Los Angeles, CA 90046
323-653-0303
www.therugcompany.info
Rugs from designers including Paul Smith, Marni, and Matthew Williamson

Eco materials

Livingreen
218 Helena Avenue,
Santa Barbara, CA 93101
805-966-1319
www.livingreen.com
Smart, new, and healthy alternative solutions to standard materials, selected to improve indoor air quality and produce less toxic construction waste. Products made from highly renewable natural resources or recycled materials

Natural Home Design Center
P.O. Box 1677,
Sebastopol, CA 95473
707-571-1229
www.naturalhomeproducts.com
Sustainable, natural, and beautiful building products with the highest quality for your health

Furnishing fabrics and textiles

Bute Fabrics Ltd
Textile Solutions, 7 Cove Circle,
Marion, MA 02738
508-748-9588
www.butefabrics.com
Contemporary upholstery fabrics, projects include collaborations with designers such as Matthew Hilton, Jasper Morrison, and Tom Dixon

Contemporary Cloth
P.O. Box 733,
Willoughby, Ohio 44094-0733
866-415-3372
www.contemporarycloth.com
Website for contemporary, retro modern, reproduction, and hand-silk-screen textiles

Kvadrat Ltd
Maharam, 251 Park Avenue South,
New York, NY 10010
800-645-3943
www.kvadrat.dk
Curtain and upholstery fabrics, from designers such as Arne Jacobsen and Ray Eames

Furniture designers and makers

Damian Velasquez
312 Stanford Drive,
Alburquerque, New Mexico 87107
505-884-5200
www.moderhandcrafted.com
Modern hand-crafted furniture

Maxwell Pinborough Ltd
398–399 Mentmore Terrace,
London E8 3PH, UK
+44 (0)20 8525 5522
www.maxwellpinborough.com
Bespoke contemporary furniture and interiors

RG Furniture Design
489 7th Avenue # 4,
Brooklyn, NY 11215
718-383-7174
www.rgrgfurnituredesign.com
Hand-made furniture crafted from reclaimed antique lumber

Victoria Hagan Interiors
654 Madison Avenue,
New York, NY 10021
212-888-3241
www.victoriahagan.com
Traditional and modern furniture, fabric, and accessories

Furniture and home accessories

Atlantico
33 Greene Street,
New York, NY 10013
212-625-1039
www.atlantico-usa.com
Modern solid wood furniture

Bloomingdales
59th Street & Lexington Avenue,
1000 3rd Avenue,
New York, NY 10022
212-705-2000
www.bloomingdales.com
Contemporary furniture and lighting

Bo Concept
180 Pulaski Street,
Bayonne, NJ 07002
201-433-4461
www.boconcept.us
Elegant minimal furniture and modular shelving

Carl Hansen and Son, Inc.
462 Wellington Street West, Suite 502,
Toronto, ON M5V 1E3
416-572-4073
www.carlhansen.com

Cassina
155 East 56th Street,
New York, NY 10022
212-245-2121
www.cassina.com

The Cherner Chair Company
P.O. Box 2689,
Westport, CT 06880
866-243-7637
www.chernerchair.com
The sole licensor of Norman Cherner design furniture, including chairs, stools, and tables

The Conran Shop
407 East 59th Street,
Between First and York Avenue,
New York, NY 10022
212-755-9079
www.conran.com

Flexform
Nova Studio International, LLC
150 East 58th Street,
New York, NY 10155
212-421-1220
www.flexformusa.com

Fritz Hansen
22 Wooster Street,
New York, NY 10013
212-219-3226
www.fritzhansen.com
Contemporary furniture from international designers including Arne Jacobsen

Herman Miller
855 East Main Avenue,
P.O. Box 302,
Zeeland, Michigan 9464-0302
616-654-3000
www.hermanmiller.com

highbrowfurniture.com
2110 8th Avenue,
South Nashville, Tennessee
888-329-0219
www.highbrowfurniture.com
Authentic iconic modern furniture

Ikea
2149 Fenton Parkway,
San Diego, CA 92108
619-563-4532
www.ikea.com
Units and accessories. Excellent value for smart Scandinavian design. Branches nationwide

Knoll International
76 9th Avenue, Floor 11,
New York, NY 10011
212-343-4000
www.knollint.com

Krypton
707 Monroe Way,
Placentia, CA 92870
714-577-0219
www.krypton1.com

Ligne Roset
Roset USA Corp.
665 Broadway, Suite 800,
New York, NY 10012
212-358-9204
www.ligne-roset-usa.com

Macy's Furniture Gallery
98 Richmond Hill Road,
Staten Island, NY 10314
718-494-4094
www.macys.com

MDF Italia
Via Morimondo 5/7,
20143 Milan, Italy
+39 0281804001 (for suppliers)
www.mdfitalia.it
Sleek Italian furniture

Mobelform
1855 Griffin Road B408
Dania Beach, FL 33004
954-922-7234
www.mobelform.com
Collections of contemporary furniture, lighting, and accessories

Modernica
57 Green Street,
New York, NY 10012
212-219-1303
7366 Beverly Boulevard,
Los Angeles, CA 90036
323-933-0383
555 Franklin Street,
Chicago, IL 60610
312-222-1808
www.modernica.net
Re-edition furniture and accessories, including George Nelson bubble lamps, Isamu Noguchi coffee tables and Charles and Ray Eames chairs

NY Loft
6 West 20th Street,
New York, NY 10011
212-206-7400
www.nyloft.net

R Twentieth-century Design
82 Franklin Street,
New York, NY 10013
212-343-7979
www.r20thcentury.com
Contemporary designs including furniture, accessories, and lighting

Relish
433 NW 10th Street,
Portland, OR 97209
503-227-3779
www.relishstyle.com
Contemporary home accessories

RETRO@HOME
3811 San Pablo Avenue,
Emeryville, CA 94608
510-658-6600
www.retroathome.com

Retromodern
805 Peachtree Street
Atlanta, GA 30308
404-724-0093
www.retromodern.com

Room and Board
55 East Ohio Street,
Chicago, IL 60611
312-222-0970
www.roomandboard.com

Senzatempo
1655 Meridian Avenue,
Miami Beach, FL 331939
305-534-5588
www.senzatempo.com

Vitra
149 5th Avenue,
New York, NY 10010
212-539-1900
www.vitra.com
Re-edition furniture. Designers stocked include Alvar Aalto and Richard Neutra

Weego Home
2939 Main Street,
Santa Monica, CA 90405
800-659-3346
www.weegohome.com
Simple and elegant classical modern furniture and home accessories

2Modern
108 Topaz Avenue,
Newport Beach, CA 92662
888-222-4410
www.2modern.com

Garden furniture and lighting

See also listings under Furniture and home accessories

Modern Outdoor
15952 Strathern Street,
Van Nuys, CA 91406
818-785-0171
www.modernoutdoor.com

Thos. Baker
203 Parfitt Way SW, Suite 210,
Bainbridge Island, WA 98110
877-855-1900
www.thosbaker.com
Good value outdoor furniture made from sustainable materials

YLighting
888-888-449
www.ylighting.com
Fine modern lighting with a good range of outdoor lighting

Infloor heating

Infloor
Hamel, MN
800-608-0562
www.infloor.com

Kitchen furniture and fixtures

Big Chill
877-842-3269
e-mail: info@bigchillfridge.com
www.bigchillfridge.com
Retro refrigerators and stoves

Boffi
1344 4th Street,
Santa Monica, CA 90401
310-458-9300
www.boffi.com

CaesarStone
11830 Sheldon Street
Sun Valley CA, 91352
818-394-6000
www.caesarstoneus.com
Quartz surfaces

GE
800-626-2005
www.geappliances.com
Large range of kitchen appliances

Kraftmaid
P.O. Box 1055,
15535 South State Avenue,
Middlefield, OH 44062
888-562-7744
www.kraftmaid.com
Affordable fitted kitchens with a modern range

Miele (Dallas Showroom)
1700 Oak Lawn Avenue, Suite 200
Dallas, TX 75207
800-843-7231
www.miele.com
Smart kitchens and appliances

NY Loft
6 West 20th Street,
New York, NY 10011
212-206-7400
www.nyloft.net

Scavolini
Via Risara, 60/70-74/78
61025 Montelabbate (PU), Italy
+39 07214431
E-mail: contact@scavolini.com
www.scavolini.com
Modern Italian fitted kitchens

Siemens
Wittelsbacherplatz 2,
D-80333 Munich, Germany
+49 89 636 00
www.siemens.com
Large range of kitchen appliances and accessories

Zephyr Corporation
395 Mendell Street,
San Francisco, CA 94124
888-880-3368
www.zephyronline.com
High-performance kitchen ventilation

Leather flooring, walling, and furniture

Bill Amberg
www.billamberg.com
Bespoke leather furniture, floor and wall tiles

GreenFloors
3170 Draper Drive,
Fairfax, VA 22031
703-352-8300
www.greenfloors.com
Recycled 100% leather floor tiles

Interior Leather Surfaces
5 Lakeshore Close,
Sleepy Hollow, NY 10591
877-231-2100
www.interiorsurfaces.com
www.leatherdecorating.com
Finest quality leather tiles for floors, walls, and ceilings

Lighting

Artemide Inc.
46 Greene Street,
New York, NY 10013
212-925-1588
or
9006 Beverly Boulevard,
West Hollywood, CA 90048
310-888-4099
or
855 Montgomery Street,
San Francisco, CA 94133
415-393-9955
or
277 Giralda Avenue,
Coral Gables, FL 33134
305-444-5800
www.artemide.com
Renowned Italian lighting designs

Europebynet.com
38 Dover Street
London W1S 4NL
888-660-4870
www.europebynet.com
Modern lighting fom European designers, including Ingo Maurer

Flos Inc.
200 McKay Road
Huntington Station, NY 11746
516-549-2745
www.flos.net
Contemporary lighting from designers such as Achille Castiglioni, Philippe Starck, and Jasper Morrison

Mathmos
www.mathmos.com
Famous for the Lava Lamp, but there's more besides

YLighting
333 Washington Boulevard # 351,
Marina del Rey, CA 90292
866-428-9289
www.ylighting.com
Stockists of contemporary lighting designs, including Artemide, Flos, Fontana Arte, Foscarini, and George Nelson bubble lamps

Metal and metalworkers

Couturier Iron Craft, Inc.
5050 West River Drive
Comstock Park, MI 49321-0308
616-784-6780 / 800-670-6123
www.couturierironcraft.com
Custom-made architectural metal products including column covers, domes, trellises, fascias, towers, medallions, benches, light fixtures, staircases, and railings. Produced in conjunction with architects, engineers, and contractors to provide high quality products

DSI Architectural Products, Inc.
760 South 104th Street,
Broomfield, CO 80020
303-665-8303 / 800-951-7727
www.dsiarchitecturalproducts.com
Stainless steel and copper stairways that are both durable and creatively designed.

Metal flooring

Carina Works, Inc.
8711 Burnet Road, Suite H-98,
Austin, TX 78757
800-504-5095
www.carinaworks.com
Metal flooring planks in a satin matte finish, as well as metal tiles for walls and metal kitchen countertops

Natural fiber floor coverings

Ceres Natural Flooring
55 Mall Drive,
Commack, NY 11725
888-377-8801
www.cerescork.com
Renewable and recyclable cork flooring, as well as recycled rubber flooring

Cork Innovations
2852 Willamette Street #133,
Eugene, OR 97405
888-205-2128
www.corkinnovations.com
Natural cork flooring and, including floating floors, floor tiles, and wall tiles

Gerbert Limited
715 Fountain Avenue, P.O. Box 4944,
Lancaster, PA 17604-4944
717-299-5035 or 800-828-9461
www.gerbetltd.com
*Renewable and recyclable cork plank
flooring, as well as rubber and vinyl flooring*

Natural Area Rugs
8306 Wilshire Boulevard # 4500,
Beverly Hills, CA 90211
800-661-7847
www.naturalarearugs.com
*Natural floorcoverings, including sisal,
seagrass, jute, and bamboo rugs*

Natural Cork, LLC
1710 North Leg Court
Augusta, Georgia 30909
706-733-6120
www.naturalcork.com
Cork products for floors and walls

Office furniture

*See listings under Furniture and
home accessories*

Paint

Benjamin Moore & Co.
51 Chestnut Ridge Road
Montvale, NJ 07645
800-344-0400
www.benjaminmoore.com
*On-line order service available for all
Benjamin Moore paints and the Color
Preview Professional Color Selector. Also
offers a color matching service. Visit the
website to find your local dealer*

Keim Mineral Systems
Cohalan Company
62 Port Lewes
Lewes, DE 19958
302-344-9094
www.keimmineralsystems.com
*Range of long-life, color-fast masonry
paints available with technical and color
consultation*

**National Paint and Coatings Association
(NPCA)**
1500 Rhode Island Avenue
NW Washington, DC 20005
202-462-6272
www.paint.org
*General information on paint. List of
manufacturers and suppliers throughout
the US*

Paint and Wallcovering Contractor (PWC)
107 West Pacific Avenue
St Louis, MO 63119-3776
314-961-6644
www.paintstore.com
*General information on paint. List of
manufacturers and suppliers throughout
the US*

Plastics and acrylics

Yemm & Hart
1417 Madison, Suite 308
Marquand, MI 63655-9153
573-783-5434
Recycled plastic sheets and panels

Stainless steel worktops and backsplashes

Carina Works, Inc.
8711 Burnet Road, Suite H-98,
Austin, TX 78757
800-504-5095
www.carinaworks.com
*Stainless steel sinks and worktops in any
size and shape. Also backsplashes, panels,
cabinets, drawer units and sanitary appliances*

Stone flooring, tiles, and countertops

Bisazza
42 Greene Street
New York, NY 10013
212-334-7130
www.bisazza.it
Ceramic flooring including mosaics

Paris Ceramics
150 East 58th Street, 7th Floor
New York, NY 10155
212-644-2782
www.parisceramics.com
*Wide range of new and reclaimed tile
flooring available including limestone
and mosaic*

Stoves and fireplaces

European Home
307 Porter Street,
Melrose, MA 02176
781-662-1110
www.europeanhome.com
*Contemporary fireplaces, gas stoves, bath
fixtures, and architectural surface material*

Wittus
40 Westchester Avenue,
Pound Ridge, NY 10576
914-764-5679
www.wittus.com
Danish stoves and contemporary fireplaces

Synthethic floor coverings

Ceres Natural Flooring
55 Mall Drive,
Commack, NY 11725
888-377-8801
www.cerescork.com
*Renewable and recyclable cork flooring,
as well as recycled rubber flooring*

Vintage furniture and home accessories

Century Design Ltd
1531 Washington Ave # 9E,
St. Louis, MO 63103
314-588-8800
314-721-3719
www.centurydesignltd.com

Century Modern
2928 Main Street,
Dallas, TX 75226
214-651-9200
www.centurymodern.com
*Features mid-century modern furniture and
accessories by architects and reknown
designers from around the world*

Lost City Arts
18 Cooper Square,
New York, NY 10003
212-375-0500
www.lostcityarts.com
*A leading source of twentieth-century design
furniture, lighting, and accessories*

Modernica
57 Green Street
New York, NY 10012
212-219-1303
www.modernica.net
*Re-edition furniture and accessories,
including bubble lamps and contemporary
designs. Designers stocked include George
Nelson and Charles and Ray Eames*

Modern Vintage
Long Beach, CA
562-989-8500
www.modernvintagefurniture.com
*Specialists in contemporary furniture, from
the 1950s through to the present day*

Swankarama
107 West Hargett Street,
Raleigh, NC 27601
562-989-8500
www.swankarama.com
*Twentieth-century modern antiques and
furniture*

Wood flooring, paneling, and countertops

Authentic Pine Floors, Inc.
4042 Highway
42 Locust Grove, GA 30248
770-957-6038
www.authenticpinefloors.com
*Wide range of pine flooring available
including new and reclaimed timber*

John Cox Lumber Company
P.O. Box 9466,
Houston, TX 77261-9466
713-923-9423
www.coxhardware.com

**National Wood Flooring Association
(NWFA)**
16388 Westwoods Business Park
Ellisville, MO 63021
800-422-4556 (US)
800-848-8824 (Can)
www.nwfa.org
www.woodfloors.org
*General information on timber. List of
manufacturers and suppliers throughout
the US*

Wood decking

Archadeck
2112 West Laburnum Avenue
Suite 100, Richmond, VA 23227
800-722-4668
www.archadeck.com
*Range of pre-built and custom-made
decking available. Outlets across the US
and Canada*

Decks USA
97 Karago Avenue, Suite 5,
Boardman, OH 44512-5977
330-726-5540
www.decksusa.com

Index

Picture credits

The publisher has made every effort to trace the copyright holders, architects, and designers of the pictures used in this book. We apologize in advance for any unintentional omissions and would be pleased to insert the appropriate acknowledgment in any subsequent edition.

2 Photographer Tim Evan-Cook/Red Cover/Designers Marta Pan and André Wogenscky; **4** Photographer Hayo Heye/Schöner Wohnen/Camera Press/Designer Siw Matzen; **11** Photographer Peter Cook/View/Architect Feeny Mallindine Architects; **12 bottom right** Photographer Matthew Donaldson for Cassina; **13** Photographer Åke E:son Lindman/Architect Shideh Shaygan; **14 bottom left** Photographer James Merrell for SCP; **15** Photographer Anthony Cotsifas/Architect Smith-Miller + Hawkinson Architects; **16 top centre and top right** Photographer Mario Carrieri for Cassina; **17** Photographer Craig Hudson/Architect George Elphick at Elphick Proome Architects; **18 top right** Vitra Design Museum; **19** Photographer Åke E:son Lindman/Architect Anna von Schewen Design & Architecture; **21** Photographer Matt Chisnall/Architect Simon Allford at Allford Hall Monaghan Morris; **23** Photographer Åke E:son Lindman/Architect Magnus Ståhl Architect; **24 top right** Vitra Design Museum; **24 bottom left** Vitra Design Museum; **25** Photographer Philip Bier/View/Architect David Bishop at Bluebottle; **26 middle centre** Photographer Aldo Ballo for Cassina; **26 bottom right** Photographer Oliviero Venturi for Cassina; **27** Photographer Richard Glover/View/Architect Pablo Uribe; **29** Photographer Alan Williams/Architect A-EM Architects; **31** Photographer Andreas von Einsiedel/Architect Featherstone Associates; **33** Photographer Peter Cook/View/Architect Fiona Mclean at Mclean Quinlan; **37** Photographer Graham Atkins Hughes for *ELLE Decoration UK*/Architect Denton Corker Marshall Architects; **38 top second right** Photographer Andrea Zani for Cassina; **38 top right** Herman Miller, Inc; **38 centre left** Herman Miller, Inc; **39** Photographer Åke E:son Lindman/Architect Claesson Koivisto Rune; **40 top right** Photographer Andrea Zani for Cassina; **41** Photographer Nicholas Kane/arcaid.co.uk/Architect David Mikhail Architects; **43** Photographer Andreas von Einsiedel/Architect John Crummay & Robin Rout; **44 top left** Photographer Andrea Zani for Cassina; **44 bottom right** Photographer F Obbiettivo for Cassina; **45** Photographer Edmund Sumner/View/Architect Plastik Architects; **46 top right** Photographer Aldo Ballo for Cassina; **47** Photographer Andreas von Einsiedel/Architect Featherstone Associates & Dominic Ash; **49** Photographer Pernille Schlosser/Designer Heine Design; **51** Photographer James Silverman/Architect Wahlström & Steijner Architects; **55** Photographer Jonathan Pile/Architect Project Orange; **57** Photographer James Silverman/Architect Rahel Belatchew Lerdell; **59** Photographer Bertrand Limbour/Camera Press/*Marie Claire Maison*/Architect Etienne van den Berg; **61** Photographer Henry Wilson/Red Cover/Architect Nick McMahon; **63** Photographer Winfried Heinze/Red Cover/Architect Tonkin Liu; **64 top second right** Vitra Design Museum; **65** Architect KSR Architects; **67** Photographer James Winspear/View/Architect Consarc Architects with Bluestone Kitchens; **69** Photographer Dan Tobin Smith/Camera Press/*Marie Claire Maison*/Architect Ann Boyd Design; **71** Photographer Peter Cook/View/Architect Paul Mullins Associates; **73** Photographer Edmund Sumner/View/Architect Ash Sakula Architects; **77** Photographer Graham Atkins Hughes for *ELLE Decoration UK*/Architect Denton Corker Marshall Architects; **79** Photographer Åke E:son Lindman/Architect Claesson Koivisto Rune; **81** Photographer James Silverman/Architect Rahel Belatchew Lerdell; **83** Photographer Jonathan Pile/Architect Project Orange; **85** Photographer James Silverman/Architect Phil Simmons at Simmons Interiors; **87** Photographer Andreas von Einsiedel/Architect Groupe l'Arche with Wessel von Loringhoven at CasaNova; **89** Photographer Philippe Ruault/Architect Jean Nouvel; **91** Photographer Richard Glover/View/Architect Form Design Architecture; **93** Photographer Alexandre Weinberger/Camera Press/Designer Philippe Starck; **95** Photographer Matt Chisnall/Architect Simon Allford at Allford Hall Monaghan Morris; **97** Photographer Mark York/Red Cover/Architect Alison Brooks Architects; **99** Photographer Steve Stephens/Luchford/Architect Fox Linton Associates; **103** Photographer Åke E:son Lindman/Architect Harry Elson Architect; **105** Photographer Richard Bryant/arcaid.co.uk/Architect Terry Farrell & Partners for Berkeley/Designer Tara Bernerd at Target Living; **106 centre right** Product Hang-it-all/Designers Charles & Ray Eames (1953)/Photographer Andreas Sütterlin for Vitra Design Museum; **107** Photographer James Silverman/Architect Rene Dekker; **109** Photographer Richard Glover/View/Architect DSP Architects; **110 bottom right** Photographer Oliviero Venturi for Cassina; **111** Photographer Graham Atkins Hughes for *ELLE Decoration UK*/Furnished by Atomic Interiors (0115 941 5577); **113** Photographer Jonathan Pile/Architect Project Orange; **115** Photographer Chris Gascoigne/View/Architect John Kerr Associates; **117** Photographer Habitat/Red Cover/Architect Marco Bezzoli, Michael Borgstrom & Adi Goren at architecture dot com; **119** Photographer Bo Bedre/Architect Knud Holscher; **120 top left** Photographer Oliviero Venturi for Cassina; **121** Photographer Luke White for *ELLE Decoration UK*/Architect Robert Dye at Robert Dye Associates; **125** Photographer Richard Croft/IPC/*Living etc*/Architect Berthold Lubetkin/Designer Ou Baholyodhin Studio; **127** Photographer Tom Scott/Architect Grut Partnership & Toh Shimazaki Architecture; **128 top left** Photographer Oliviero Venturi for Cassina; **129** Photographer Christian Richters/Architect Francine Houben at Mecanoo; **131** Photographer James Balston/Arcblue/Architect Rainer Spehl; **132 bottom centre** Photographer Bitetto Chimenti for Cassina; **132 bottom right** Photographer Aldo Ballo for Cassina; **133** Photographer Werner Huthmacher/Artur/Architect Augustin + Frank Architekten; **135** Vitsoe Design Service; **137** Photographer Tom Scott/Architect Mary Manatiy at Marston Manatiy Design; **138 centre second right** Herman Miller, Inc; **139** Photographer Mikael Lindén/Architect Haroma Partners; **143** Photographer Clive Nicols Garden Pictures/Designer Nina Thalinson at Lust & Fägring; **145** Photographer Clive Nicols Garden Pictures/Designer Stephen Woodhams; **147** Photographer David Clerihew/IPC/*Living etc*/Designer Karena Batstone Design & Helen Tindale at Reversed Out; **149** Photographer Andreas von Einseidel/Designer Candy and Candy; **151** Photographer Clive Nicols Garden Pictures/Designer Joe Swift and Thamasin Marsh at The Plant Room.

Acknowledgments

First, I would like to thank every architect and designer who has contributed to this book—without your inspiring work this project would have been impossible. I'd also like to thank the team at Quadrille: Alison Cathie, Jane O'Shea and Helen Lewis, editor Lisa Pendreigh for her inexhaustible enthusiasm and scrupulous attention to detail, picture researcher Helen Stallion for scouring the globe for fantastic projects, and, of course, designers Ros Holder and Sue Storey for a great-looking book that we can all be proud of.

page 2 Saint Rémy home of sculptor Martha Pan and architect André Wogensky with classic Series 7 chairs in black by Arne Jacobsen.
page 4 Tranquil interior in neutral stone and white colours with a courageous aubergine-coloured wall mural of the desert by Hamburg designer Siw Matzen.

Editorial Director Jane O'Shea
Creative Director Helen Lewis
Project Editor Lisa Pendreigh
Americanizer Eleanor Van Zandt
Designers Ros Holder and Sue Storey
Picture Researcher Helen Stallion
Production Director Vincent Smith
Production Controller Rebecca Short

First published in 2004 by
Quadrille Publishing Limited
Alhambra House
27–31 Charing Cross Road
London WC2H 0LS

Text © Fay Sweet 2004
Design and layout © Quadrille Publishing Limited 2004

British Library Cataloguing-in-Publication Data
A catalogue record for this book is available from the British Library.

ISBN 1-84400-120-2

Printed in Singapore

The publisher has made every effort to ensure that the website information given in this book is correct. Any changes to website addresses are not the responsibility of the publisher.